Highlights

T0182721

brainPLAY
FUNNIEST
PUZZLES
EVER

BOOKS FOR PUZZLE PEOPLE

Kid tested by
Lila
Age 9

HIGHLIGHTS PRESS
Honesdale, Pennsylvania

BE LOGICAL

Solve this sudoku puzzle by making sure each row, column, and 2 x 3 box has one of each fruit or veggie. Fill in the squares by drawing or writing the number of each picture.

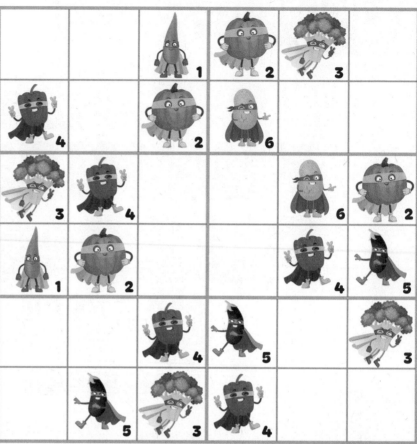

THINK ABOUT IT

Which foods can be piled up?

If a food truck came to your neighborhood, what would you want it to serve?

What topping would you be surprised to see on a pizza?

LOL

TICKLE YOUR FUNNY BONE

WHAT KIND OF MILK IS USED TO MAKE SWISS CHEESE?

HOLE MILK.

The WHOLE ENCHILADA always contains corn.

DO A WORD WORKOUT

Are each of these wacky food idioms true or false?

If you always SPILL THE BEANS, you are extra clumsy.

To GO BANANAS is to become super angry or excited.

The BIG CHEESE is the largest wheel of cheddar at the deli.

Someone who is as busy as POPCORN ON A SKILLET is constantly active or occupied.

WHAT IS THIS?

TEST YOUR EYESIGHT

what's wrong?
WACKY cafeteria

Which things in this picture are silly? It's up to you!

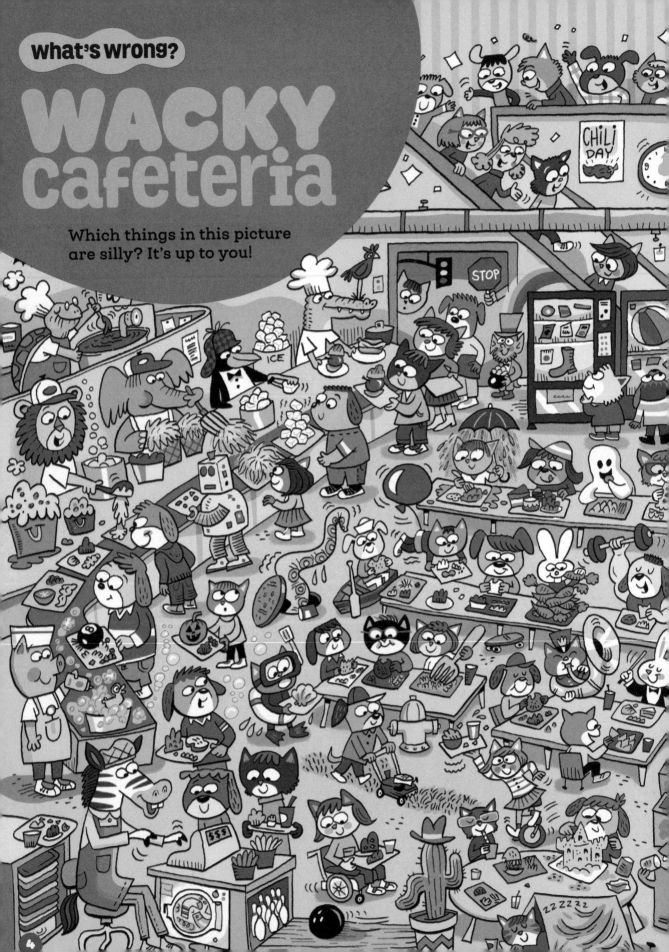

A Group of . . .

Each "if" statement will give you a letter and tell you where to put it. Fill in all the letters, and you will have your answer—no ifs, ands, or buts!

Why do giraffes have long necks?

Because their feet smell.

1. If a group of zebras is called a *razzle*, number one is an **I**. If it's called a *dazzle*, it's an **A**.

2. If a group of apes is called a *shrewdness*, number two is a **G**. If it's called a *judgment*, it's an **O**.

3. If a group of giraffes is called a *chasm*, number three is an **E**. If it's called a *tower*, it's an **I**.

4. If a group of parrots is called a *hullabaloo*, number four is an **N**. If it's called a *pandemonium*, it's an **R**.

5. If a group of hyenas is called a *chortle*, number five is a **P**. If it's called a *cackle*, it's an **F**.

6. If a group of hippos is called a *bloat*, number six is a **C**. If it's called a *float*, it's a **B**.

7. If a group of porcupines is called a *prickle*, number seven is a **J**. If it's called a *bristle*, it's a **T**.

8. If a group of flamingos is called a *flamboyance*, number eight is an **M**. If it's called a *ferocity*, it's a **Y**.

What do you get when two giraffes collide?

__ __ __ __ - __ __ __ __ __ __
1   2   3   4   1   5   5   3   6   7   1   8

PIRATE PLUNGE

FIND THESE OBJECTS IN THE SCENE.

banana
cupcake
eyeglasses

firefighter's helmet
glove
hockey stick

paper airplane
ring
shoe

slice of pizza
suitcase
wedge of lime

A Thank-You _____
noun

This is best played with friends or family. Without letting them read the story, ask for the words or phrases under the blanks. (For example, the first thing you'll ask for is a friend's first name.) After you've filled in all the blanks, read the story out loud.

Dear _____ ,
    FRIEND'S FIRST NAME

Thanks for my birthday present, the brand-new Ultra-_____
                                                        NOUN

-o-Matic Micro Plus! I've wanted one of those for _____ days!
                                                    SMALL NUMBER

I just went out and bought the _____ AA batteries it
                                  LARGE NUMBER

needs and turned it on. Wow! It purrs just like a(n) _____
                                                        ADJECTIVE

_____ _____ when it's on " _____
    COLOR   WILD ANIMAL   ADJECTIVE

mode." There was a short blast that destroyed our _____ ,
                                                    PIECE OF LIVING ROOM FURNITURE

but otherwise it's operating smoothly. I plugged our _____
                                                        APPLIANCE

into it. In just a few seconds, out came five pounds of _____ !
                                                            SNACK FOOD

I was so happy! I had no idea that this new _____ was so
                                                NOUN

different from the _____-o-Matic Micro!
                        NOUN

I can't wait until your birthday, when I can get you something just as

_____ !
    ADJECTIVE

Thanks again,

_____
    YOUR FIRST NAME

YOU'VE got to be Kitten me!

Finish these a-*mew*-sing jokes by matching each riddle with its punch line.

1 What happened when the cat ate a ball of yarn?

2 What do you call a cat drinking lemonade?

3 What did the cat say when he stubbed his toe?

4 What is a cat's favorite color?

5 What cats like to go bowling?

6 Where do you get a birthday present for a cat?

A *Purr*-ple.

C A sourpuss.

E She had mittens.

B "Me-OUCH!"

D Alley cats.

F From a catalog.

what kind of superhero are you?

Superheroes are brave in different ways. Take this quiz to find out which superhero you are!

Where do superheroes shop?

At the supermarket.

what is closest to your dream job?

- **A** Firefighter
- **B** Chef
- **C** Actor
- **D** Teacher

you're on a group trip to an amusement park. you say:

- **A** "Show me to the biggest roller coaster!"
- **B** "Let's check out the exhibit of spooky things!"
- **C** "Yes! A karaoke sing-off. I'm in!"
- **D** "Need a buddy? Come with us!"

AT SCHOOL, YOU'RE THE ONE WHO

- **A** makes it to the top of the climbing wall first.
- **B** loves creative projects.
- **C** always volunteers for show-and-tell.
- **D** welcomes the new kid.

which would be easiest for you?

- **A** Zip-lining through a forest.
- **B** Ordering a "mystery" food off the menu.
- **C** Pretending to be a farm animal in front of a crowd.
- **D** Sticking up for someone who's being teased.

you hardly ever

- **A** say no to a race.
- **B** make something the same way twice.
- **C** feel shy.
- **D** don't know what to say to someone.

As a superhero, you'd be known for

- **A** using strength and speed when you need to.
- **B** forging your own path.
- **C** dazzling everyone with theatrical performances.
- **D** bringing people together.

o to the letter you icked most to find our answer!

B
THE EXPLORER

You like to explore and create. Lots of people stick with the foods and places they know, but you are not afraid to try new things.

A
MAXIMUM ACTION

You enjoy going fast and don't mind some physical risk. Activities that seem scary to others are exciting to you. People admire your sense of adventure. Just don't forget your safety gear!

C
CAPTAIN SPOTLIGHT

You love to perform and are not afraid of an audience. You shine in the spotlight when all eyes are on you! Your bravery helps to keep others entertained.

D
FRIEND DEFENDER

You are confident in social situations. People feel good around you because you are a loyal friend and stand up for what's right. Good for you. That takes courage!

ring

light bulb

lollipop

hot dog

closed umbrella

glove

How does a dinosaur jump into a pool?

With a time machine.

Dino Divers

crescent moon

eyeglasses

adhesive bandage

comb

balloon

baseball

Laughter around
THE WORLD

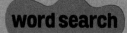

We've hidden 14 ways to say **laughter** in languages from around the world.
They are hidden up, down, across, backward, and diagonally.
Only the words in CAPITAL LETTERS are hidden.

```
P  G  L  H  W  E  S  K  A  P  C  E
M  F  A  R  C  A  A  H  L  H  U  E
X  S  C  X  J  A  A  S  W  T  S  S
K  I  H  A  D  K  L  E  I  C  E  N
H  A  E  I  H  V  R  E  P  R  U  A
K  M  N  A  E  T  F  V  G  T  M  H
I  I  K  A  H  O  J  W  U  H  L  R
M  B  C  I  K  A  T  A  K  A  T  A
S  N  N  H  E  A  S  R  G  E  U  M
E  R  I  R  E  U  W  A  F  F  W  M
G  W  D  V  E  K  C  I  O  R  N  M
I  T  J  C  J  U  O  E  U  M  A  B
```

WORD LIST

CHWERTHIN (Welsh)
DAHIK (Arabic)
GELACH (Dutch)
HANSEE (Hindi)
KAHKAHA (Turkish)
KATAKATA (Maori)
KICHEKO (Swahili)

LACHEN (German)
LAG (Afrikaans)
RIRE (French)
RISA (Spanish)
SMIKH (Ukrainian)
US-EUM (Korean)
WARAI (Japanese)

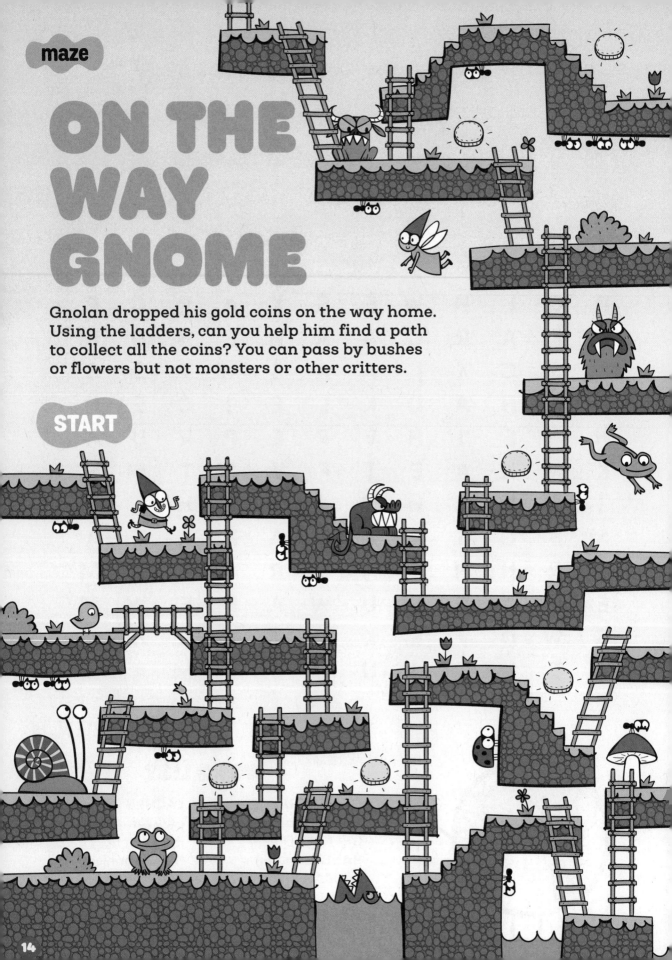

maze

ON THE WAY GNOME

Gnolan dropped his gold coins on the way home. Using the ladders, can you help him find a path to collect all the coins? You can pass by bushes or flowers but not monsters or other critters.

START

FINISH

BONUS!
Are there more ants or flowers in the scene?

15

spot the impostor

crab craze

Can you find the the lobster? How about the 12 seashells?

FACE-OFF

Every emoji should only appear once in each row, column, and 2 x 3 box. Fill in the squares by drawing or writing the number of each picture.

Why is the nose in the middle of your face?

Because it's the scenter.

1	2				3
4			5		1
	4	1	2	5	
	5	6	3	1	
6		2			5
5				6	2

17

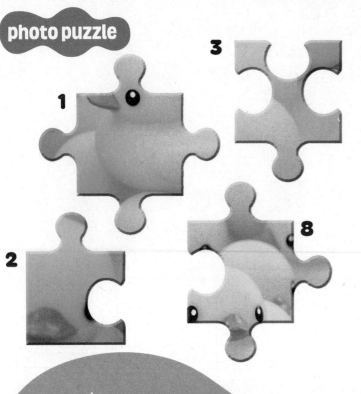

just
DUCKieS

Can you find these 8 jigsaw pieces in this photo of rubber ducks?

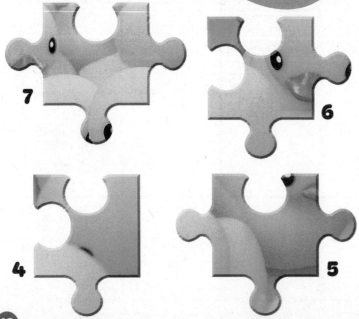

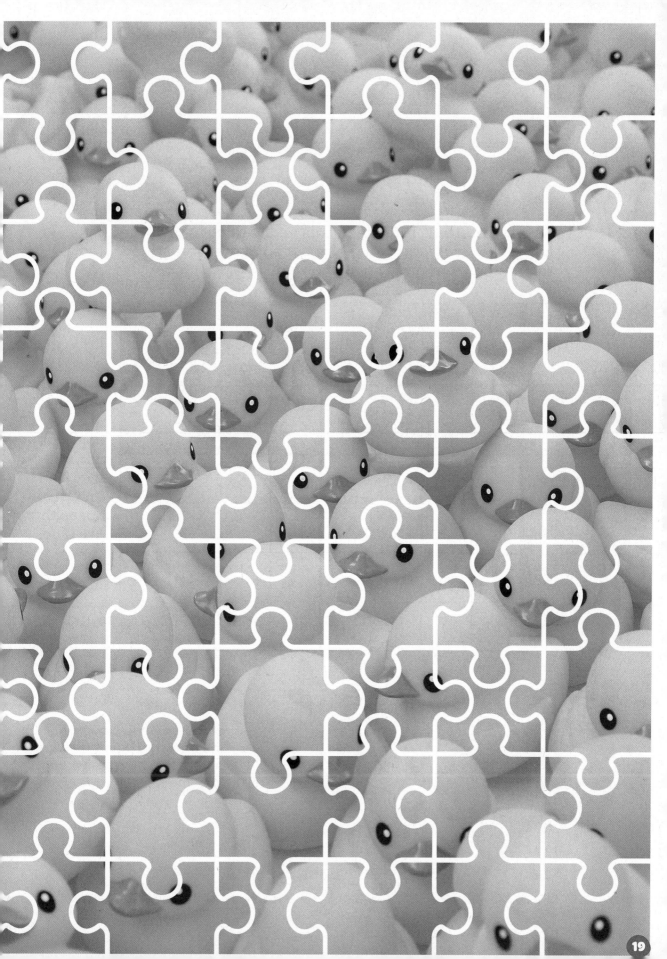

Talent SHOW

Competition was FIERCE at this year's talent show. Using the clues, can you figure out each monster's talent and what prize each one won?

	guitar solo	slime juggling	interpretive dance	self-portrait	1st	2nd	3rd	honorable mention
Blobert								
Eshriekiel								
Firegus								
Goopson								

Put an **X** in every box that can't be true and an **O** in boxes that are true.

CLUES

1 The juggler accidentally spilled some of their slime on the 3rd place monster.

2 Eshriekiel, who took 2nd place, learned to play guitar from their grandmother.

3 Blobert helped Goopson find their missing paintbrush just before the interpretive dancer took the stage.

4 Goopson placed before Firegus but after Eshriekiel.

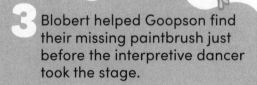

Get coordinated

Use the number pairs to solve the riddle on this grid. Move to the right to the first number and then up to the second number. Write the letter you find in each space.

HA HA !!

What do you get when you cross a duck and a calculator?

A quack-ulator.

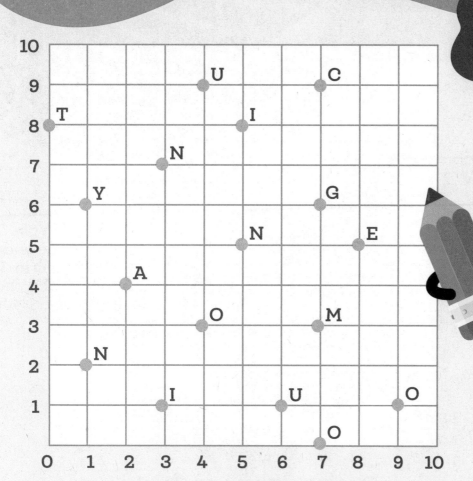

what did the student say to the calculator?

" $\overline{}$ $\overline{}$ $\overline{}$
3,1   2,4   7,3

$\overline{}$ $\overline{}$ $\overline{}$ $\overline{}$ $\overline{}$ $\overline{}$ $\overline{}$ $\overline{}$
7,9   9,1   4,9   3,7   0,8   5,8   1,2   7,6

$\overline{}$ $\overline{}$ $\overline{}$ $\overline{}$ $\overline{}$ "
4,3   5,5   1,6   7,0   6,1

brain breaks

HINT: Is this thing on?

TEST YOUR EYESIGHT

WHAT IS THIS?

A flock of geese

DO A WORD WORKOUT

Series of sharp turns

Use the clues to name words that contain the letters in **GAG.**

A small novelty device

A standard measurement

Bags for traveling

?!

THINK ABOUT IT

Do you like to have pranks played on you? WHY OR WHY NOT?

When might it be useful to know some jokes?

Is it easier to tell a joke or to listen to one? WHY?

ha ha!

HA HA !!

GEMMA: *Have you heard the joke about the spy?*
OGGIE: *No, tell me.*
GEMMA: *Sorry, I can't. It's top secret.*

STRETCH YOUR MATH SKILLS

Kiernan, Elianna, Rodrigo, and Nylah entered a pie-throwing contest. Each contestant got **10 THROWS**. Together the four friends hit the target **26 TIMES**. If Nylah made as many hits as she missed and Kiernan scored two fewer hits than Elianna but two more than Rodrigo, how many hits did each person make?

BE LOGICAL

Trace the white drawing without lifting your pencil or crossing or repeating any lines.

START

TREEHOUSE TEE-HEES

Which things in this picture are silly? It's up to you!

whooo's there?

Crack the code to fill in the knock-knock jokes. Once you know one number's letter, you can fill in that letter each time you see that number.

Say this tongue twister three times fast!
All owls howl for hours.

1

K N O C K , K N O C K .
1 2 3 4 1   1 2 3 4 1

__ __ __ , __ __ __ __ __ __ ?
5 6 3   7   8 6 9 10 9

__ __ __ .
5 6 3

__ __ __ __ __ __ ?
5 6 3   5 6 3

__ __ __ __ __ , __ __ __ __ __
11 12 11 12 2   8   1 2 3 5

__ __ __ __ __ __ __ __ __ __ !
13 3 14 7 15 3 1   9 3 5 16

2

__ __ __ __ __ , __ __ __ __ __ .
1 2 3 4 1   1 2 3 4 1

__ __ __ , __ __ __ __ __ __ ?
5 6 3   7   8 6 9 10 9

__ __ __ .
3 5 16

__ __ __ __ __ __ ?
3 5 16   5 6 3

__ __ __ __ __ __ __ __ __ __ __ __
3 5 16   2 11 17 6 8   16 3 2 17

__ __ __ __ __ __ __ __ __ !
11 5 18   7   18 5 18 1 9

25

POP THE BALLOON

FIND THESE OBJECTS IN THE SCENE.

adhesive bandage
banana
bird
bowling ball
button

candy cane
comb
crayon
drinking straw
envelope

fishhook
fried egg
glove
hockey stick
needle

paintbrush
paper clip
pen
pencil
pennant

ring
ruler
saltshaker
slice of pie
slice of pizza

tack
toothbrush
tweezers
worm
yo-yo

Tic Tac Cat

What do the groovy cats in each row (horizontally, vertically, and diagonally) have in common?

Cat Walk

Cats just LOVE walking across keyboards. Can you find 27 words in this string of letters one cat typed?

TYPEACHINTOPLOTHEREALSOMEATUNA

PLEASE EXCUSE _____
YOUR FIRST NAME

This is best played with friends or family. Without letting them read the story, ask for the words or phrases under the blanks. (For example, the first thing you'll ask for is *your first name*.) After you've filled in all the blanks, read the story out loud.

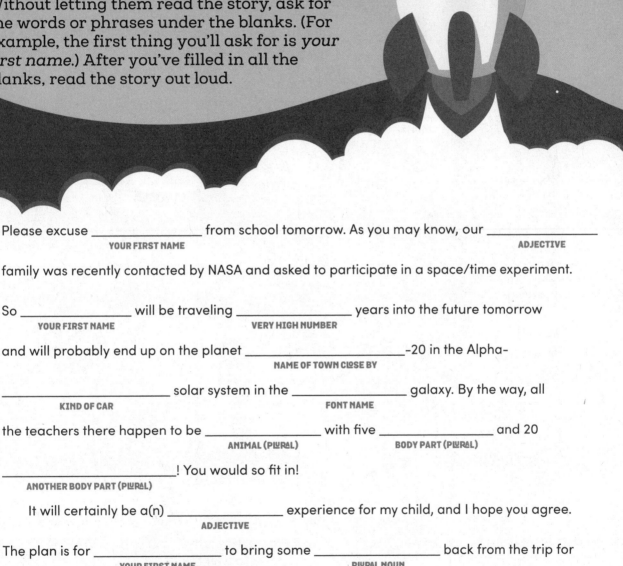

Please excuse _____ from school tomorrow. As you may know, our _____
YOUR FIRST NAME   ADJECTIVE

family was recently contacted by NASA and asked to participate in a space/time experiment.

So _____ will be traveling _____ years into the future tomorrow
YOUR FIRST NAME   VERY HIGH NUMBER

and will probably end up on the planet _____-20 in the Alpha-
NAME OF TOWN CLOSE BY

_____ solar system in the _____ galaxy. By the way, all
KIND OF CAR   FONT NAME

the teachers there happen to be _____ with five _____ and 20
ANIMAL (PLURAL)   BODY PART (PLURAL)

_____! You would so fit in!
ANOTHER BODY PART (PLURAL)

It will certainly be a(n) _____ experience for my child, and I hope you agree.
ADJECTIVE

The plan is for _____ to bring some _____ back from the trip for
YOUR FIRST NAME   PLURAL NOUN

_____-and-Tell at school. If all goes _____, _____
VERB   ADVERB   YOUR FIRST NAME

should be back in school by _____ and _____ with other students!
YEAR IN THE FUTURE   -ING VERB

Thank you.

Parent of _____
YOUR FIRST NAME

29

HOW HUngry Are YOU?

Take this quiz to help you decide what to snack on.

Ready to GOBBLE!

Just feeling a little Snacky.

NOT SUPER hungry.

Make a **FUN DRINK** instead! Try homemade lemonade or fruit-infused water.

How much time do you have?

sweet OR **salty**

Have some **FRESH FRUIT** or **YOGURT.**

what kind of bite are you looking for?

Not much. I'm not just hungry; I'm **HANGRY!**

I've got some time.

SOFT or **CHEWY**

CRISP and **CRUNCHY**

spread some nut butter or avocado on **TOAST.**

Is there an **ADULT** around who can cook with you?

YES ✓   **NO** ✗

Try a **CHEESE STICK** or **HUMMUS.**

Top with **CRACKERS** cheese and pepperoni or ham.

Have a **PICKLE.**

EW!

Do you love breakfast food?

NO ✗   **YES** ✓

Make **NACHOS.**

Make **PANCAKES!**

Fair enough! HOW about **PRETZELS** or **POPCORN?**

unidentified UFOs

UFO usually stands for Unidentified Flying Object. But each of these clues describes a different UFO! Can you identify all the matches?

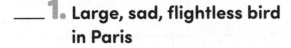

____ **1.** Large, sad, flightless bird in Paris

____ **2.** Lint-covered breakfast food

____ **3.** Lively international musical

____ **4.** Wise winged girls in the city

____ **5.** Icy and pristine Atlantic

____ **6.** Unattractive hopping robber

____ **7.** Quickly moving slime

____ **8.** Out-of-the-ordinary sea creature

____ **9.** Hilarious policeman

____ **10.** Parasol party poem

A. Ugly Frog Outlaw

B. Undisturbed Frozen Ocean

C. Unusually Fancy Octopus

D. Umbrella Festival Ode

E. Unhappy French Ostrich

F. Unbelievably Funny Officer

G. Urban Female Owls

H. Untouched Fuzzy Oatmeal

I. Urgently Flowing Ooze

J. Upbeat Foreign Opera

FUN AND GAMES

Without clues or knowing what to look for,
can you find the 21 hidden objects at the arcade?

Where do flowers sleep?

In the flower bed.

Use the clues below to fill in the boxes of this spiral—but there's a twist: The last letter of each word is also the first letter of the next word. Use the linking letters to help you spin all the way to the center. We did the first one for you.

1. Bed for a baby

4. Cover on your bed that keeps you warm

10. You take a bath in it

12. Place in the house where you sleep

18. Large, round, white object in the night sky

21. Person who likes to stay up late; also a nocturnal bird

28. Bedtime song for a baby

34. To open your mouth wide when you're tired

37. Bad dream

45. You close these to sleep

48. Animals some people count to fall asleep

52. You lay your head on it

57. What you do when you're done sleeping

62. Clothes you wear to bed

68. Soft shoes you might wear around the house

75. They twinkle in the night sky

79. Sack you sleep in while you're camping

89. What you say before going to bed: "____ night"

92. What your mind is doing while you're sleeping

PASS THE POPCORN

Find 18 differences between the two photos.

Ladder up

Start at the bottom of the castle. Use the ladders to make your way to the top. You can cross through any room with a doorway, and you can use ladders to go either up or down. **CAN YOU FIND A PATH TO THE ROOFTOP DANCE PARTY?**

BONUS! Can you also find 10 candles?

35

HEAPS of sheep

Can you find the llama? How about the 12 socks?

A-dough-rable
Doughnuts

Every doughnut should only appear once in each row, column, and 2 x 3 box. Fill in the squares by drawing or writing the number of each picture.

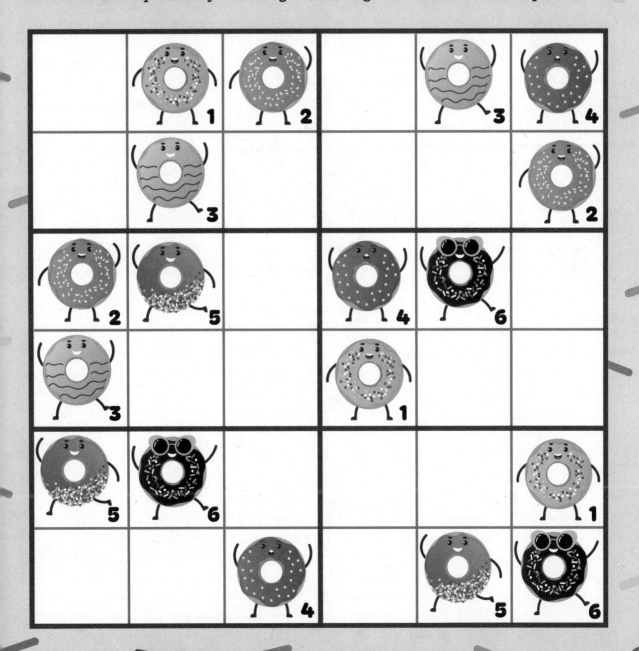

shadow
match

Take a look at the shadows
and match each one to a tasty
frozen treat below.

snails on the GO!

Use the clues below to find a path from START to FINISH. How many paths can you find?

maze

START

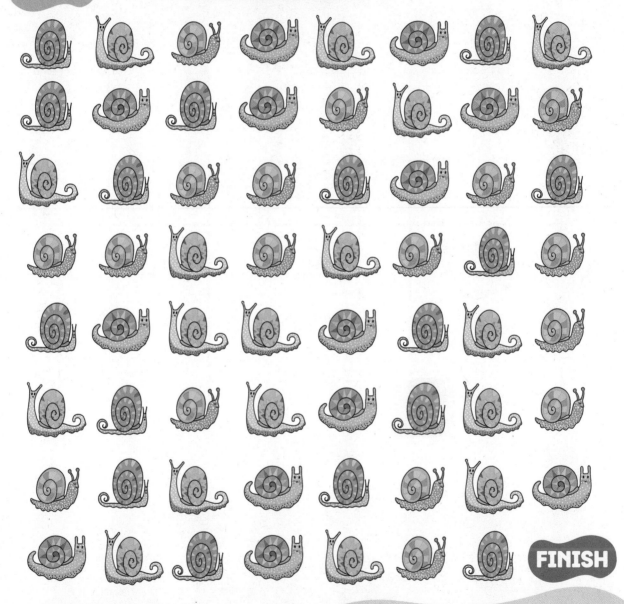

FINISH

CLUES!

 Move 1 space in any direction

 Move 1 space diagonally

 Move 2 spaces left or right

 Move 2 spaces up or down

Fan-cactus DESTINATIONS

Four cacti are vacationing in different places this winter. Using the clues, can you figure out where and when each cactus will go on vacation?

Put an **X** in every box that can't be true and an **O** in boxes that are true.

	Ice-skating in Canada	Skiing in Switzerland	Kayaking in Antarctica	Glacier hiking in Iceland	December	January	February	March
spike								
Flora								
carl								
Fluffy								

CLUES

 Hi

1 The cacti taking its trip in December doesn't like skiing.

2 Fluffy's vacation is after both Spike's and Carl's, but before Flora's.

3 Spike went shopping for skis with the cacti going glacier hiking in February.

4 Flora mapped out a few different routes to paddle on her trip.

PLAYING PATTERNS

Figure out what number comes next in each series. Then figure out which player has the highest overall score.

Player 1

A. 2, 4, 7, 11, <u>16</u>

B. 12, 10, 6, ___

C. 5, 10, 20, ___

D. 27, 9, 3, ___

E. 24, 12, 6, ___

F. 1, 5, 25, 125, ___

G. 5, 9, 7, 11, 9, ___

H. 2, 4, 16, ___

I. 18, 6, 36, 12, 72, ___

J. 50, 100, 10, 20, 2, ___

Total Score ___

Player 2

A. 4, 8, 16, ___

B. 8, 12, 18, ___

C. 60, 50, 35, ___

D. 6000, 600, 60, ___

E. 50, 100, 200, ___

F. 120, 60, 30, ___

G. 24, 28, 20, 24, ___

H. 30, 10, 60, 20, ___

I. 15, 30, 34, 68, 72, ___

J. 6, 12, 9, 15, 12, ___

Total Score ___

Why are cats so good at video games?

They have nine lives.

41

STRETCH YOUR MATH SKILLS

Which treasure chest holds the most gold?

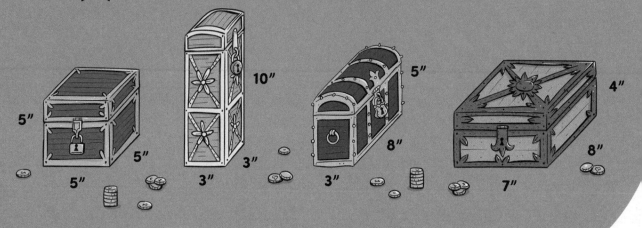

5"
5"
5"

10"
3"
3"

5"
8"
3"

4"
8"
7"

HINT:
length x width x height = volume

WHAT IS THIS?

TEST YOUR EYESIGHT

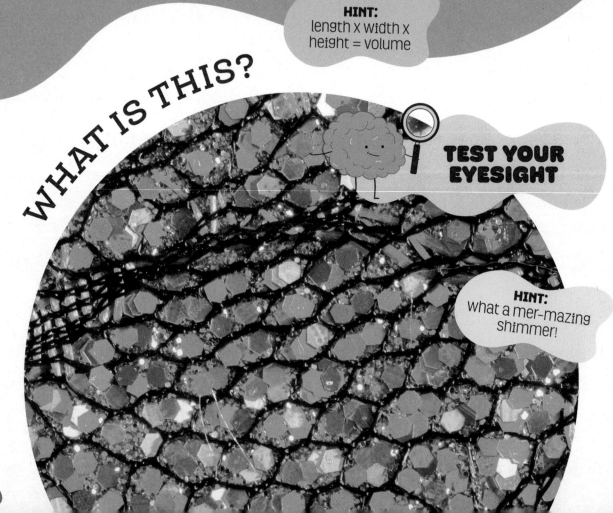

HINT:
what a mer-mazing shimmer!

DO A WORD WORKOUT

Use the clues to name words that can be made from letters in FANTASTICAL.

Coming at the end

Small amount of color

A mark that is hard to remove

A tiny, slow-moving critter

Group of actors in a play

STRETCH YOUR MIND

How many types of mythical creatures can you name in **ONE MINUTE?**

LOL

TICKLE YOUR FUNNY BONE

AAAAAACHOO!

WHAT DO YOU GET WHEN A FIRE-BREATHING DRAGON SNEEZES?

OUT OF THE WAY!

BE LOGICAL

- Moonbeam left for vacation on March 2nd.
- Nine days after leaving, she went to Sparkle Beach.
- Three days before going to the beach, she went to the Pegasus Grand Prix.
- Six days after the race, she went hiking in the Rainbow Forest.
- Two days before her hike, she visited her grandparents.

On what date did Moonbeam visit her grandparents?

what's wrong?

traffic laughs

Which things in this picture are silly? It's up to you!

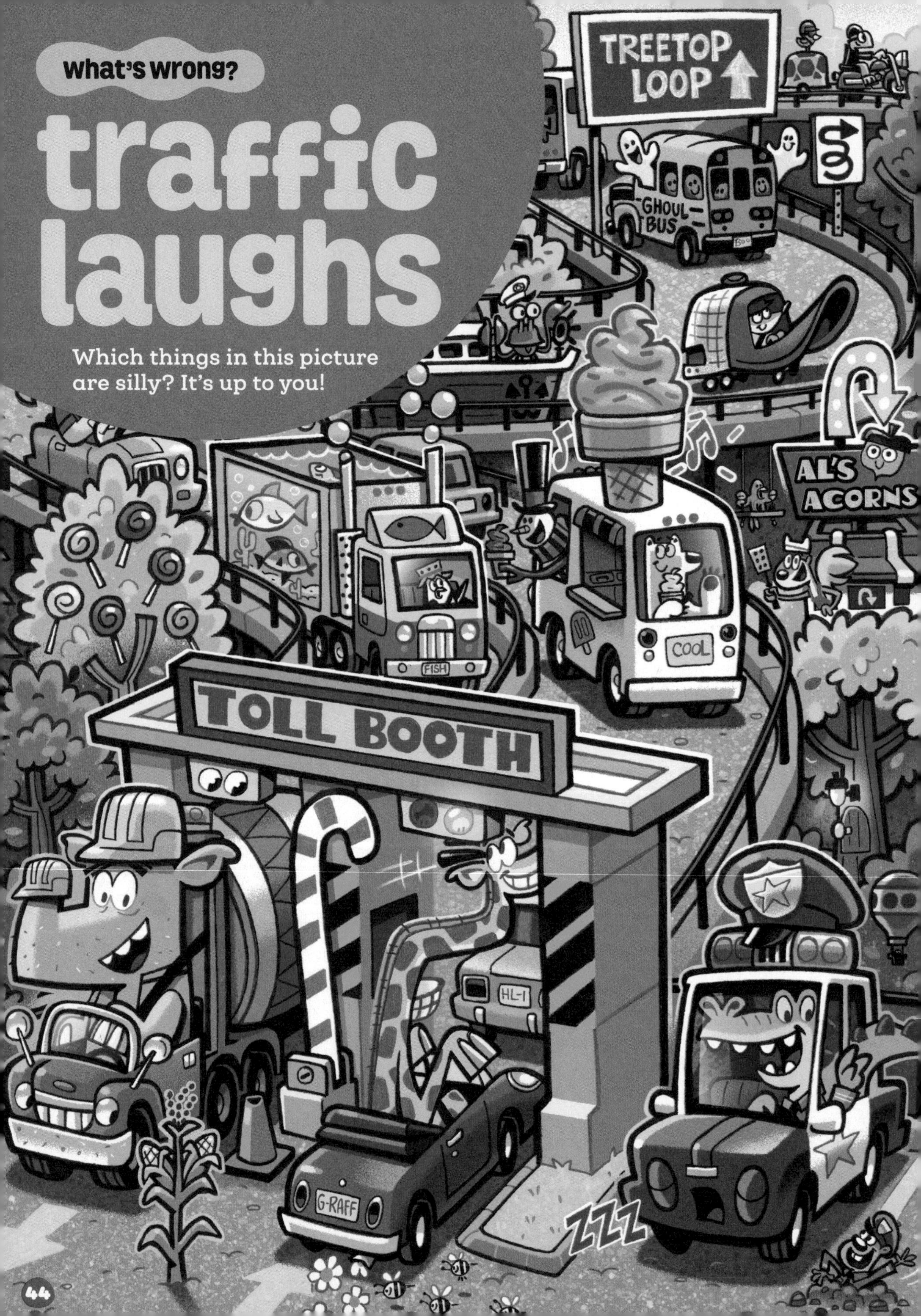

PENGUIN POOL PARTY

To answer the riddle below, start at the North (N) circle. Then move in the directions listed and write the letters you find in the correct spaces.

START

```
        N
  Y  P  T  E  E
  H  D  N  I  C
W X  O  J  W  H E
  M  O  T  L  S
  K  R  U  O  E
        S
```

WHERE DO PENGUINS LIKE TO GO SWIMMING?

1. S 1   **T**
2. SE 2   ___
3. N 2   ___

4. S 3   ___
5. W 3   ___
6. SE 1   ___
7. N 1   ___
8. NW 2   ___

9. NE 1   ___
10. S 2   ___
11. SE 2   ___
12. N 1   ___

FANCY FLAMINGOS

BONUS! can you also find the heart, baseball, envelope, and paper clip?

canoe

crescent moon

banana

octopus

mug

wedge of lemon

pennant

bowl

fishhook

ring

candy cane

toothbrush

slice of pizza

coat hanger

golf club

snake

carrot

spoon

candle

sailboat

butterfly

adhesive bandage

ruler

horseshoe

hockey stick

Tic Tac Taco

What do the spec-taco-lar tacos in each row
(horizontally, vertically, and diagonally) have in common?

RUFF

Ready for a Pet

jungle animal

This is best played with friends or family. Without letting them read the story, ask for the words or phrases under the blanks. (For example, the first thing you'll ask for is an *animal*.) After you've filled in all the blanks, read the story out loud.

Dear Parent,

We, the Pet Owners of Upper Central _____ania, do hereby certify that
YOUR CITY OR TOWN

_____ should be allowed to get a(n) _____, a(n)
YOUR FULL NAME   ANIMAL

_____, or even a dog or a cat for a pet. As you've probably heard before,
KIND OF FISH

_____ is about the greatest child we've ever met, and was recently admitted
YOUR FIRST NAME

to the University of _____. You have a(n) _____ kid! On being
PLANET   ADJECTIVE

certified, _____ promises to walk the pet every day, unless of course he/she
YOUR FIRST NAME

decides that a parent or sibling should do it. Also, _____ will teach the pet to sit,
YOUR FIRST NAME

stay, count to _____, talk, and _____. Finally, the pet shall be named
HIGH NUMBER   VERB

Lord or Lady _____ and will be allowed to sleep on a parent's
NONSENSE WORD

_____, inside the _____, or anywhere it feels like.
NOUN   APPLIANCE

Cordially,

Ivana Pettsoon

12 days of

On the 12th day of cuteness, try to find in this scene:

12 hamsters rolling,
11 bunnies hopping,
10 chipmunks chomping,
9 ponies prancing,
8 kittens mewing,
7 puppies zooming,
6 piglets playing,
5 baby goats,
4 snoozing sloths,
3 small snails,
2 hummingbirds, and
1 round little bumblebee.

heart

umbrella

mushroom

sunglasses

paintbrush

bowling ball

crescent moon

button

ice skate

purr-ito and friends

wrench

ruler

spoon

crown

kite

sailboat

road trip
cross-out

To get the answer to the riddle below, first cross out all the pairs of matching letters. Then write the remaining letters in order in the spaces below the riddle.

TT	NN	FL	OO
LL	PP	WW	XX
GG	YI	BB	RR
NG	MM	ZZ	EE
VV	TT	AA	SS
FF	HH	CA	DD
JJ	NN	UU	RP
BB	PP	NN	YY
ET	RR	LL	CC
HH	XX	DD	FF

what do you get when you cross a bird, a car, and a dog?

A

_ _ _ _ _ _ _

_ _ _ _ _ _ .

SOCK SEARCH

Find at least 15 differences between the two pictures.

pretzel path

Find your way around the pretzels, from START to FINISH.

What did the pretzel twist say to the pretzel rod?

I'd rather knot.

HA HA !!

START

finish

Which walrus?

Can you find the seal? What about the 12 fish?

SOUND EFFECTS

Every sound should only appear once in each row, column, and 2 x 3 box. Fill in the squares by drawing or writing the name of each sound.

Why did the superhero save the pickle?

Because he wanted to eat it later.

BEST FRIENDS FUR-EVER

baseball cap

crown

needle

fish

crescent moon

heart

kite

book

necktie

piece of popcorn

fishhook

bowl

shoe

spoon

WHAT'S A GIBBLE?

Can you figure out which of these are Gibbles?

These Gibbles all have features in common.

None of these are Gibbles.

animal Addition

Each animal has a unique value from 1 to 9. Can you figure out which animal represents which number? Here's a hint to help you get started: The zebra has the highest number; the unicorn has the lowest number.

Say this tongue twister three times fast! **Addison adds several sevens.**

brain breaks

TEST YOUR EYESIGHT

WHAT IS THIS?

If you have your DUCKS IN A ROW, you're organized at the start of a project.

An EARWORM is a forgettable song.

If someone tells you to HOLD YOUR HORSES, you should start searching in the barn first.

Everybody's talking about an ELEPHANT IN THE ROOM.

DO A WORD WORKOUT

Are each of these wacky animal idioms true or false?

An EAGER BEAVER describes an overly enthusiastic person.

Which reptile should go in place of each question mark so that each row and column contains all four reptiles?

Snore

RING!

Z Z z z...

TICKLE YOUR FUNNY BONE

HA HA !!

Where do fish sleep?

In waterbeds.

THINK ABOUT IT

In an **animal band**, which animal might play each instrument?

What kind of **heroic things** might animals do?

What might a bird think is **strange** about people?

SILLY SLIDES

Which things in this picture are silly? It's up to you!

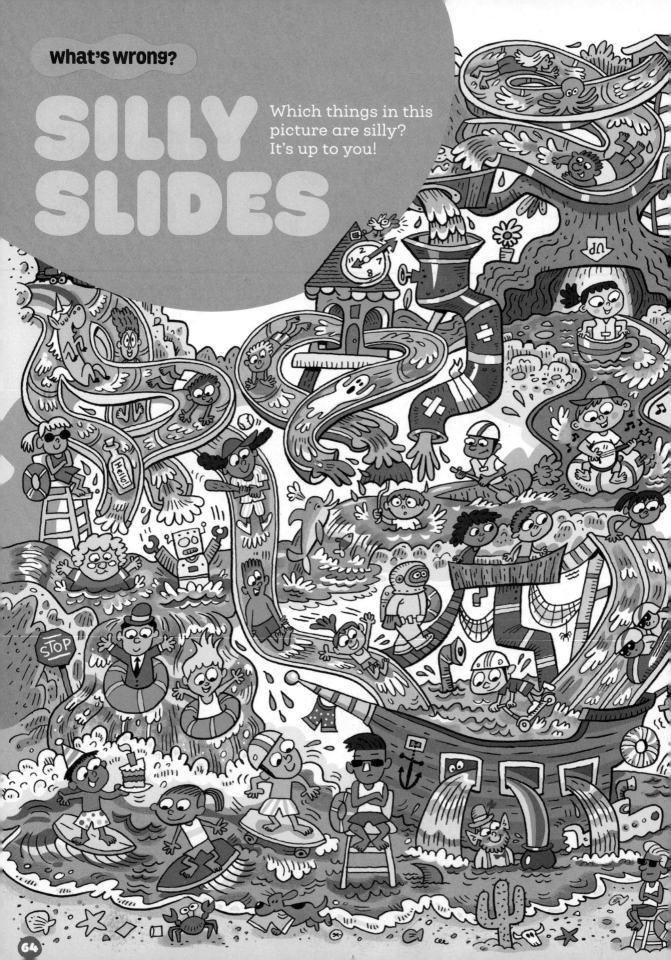

cosmic code

In the messages, each of the letters has been replaced by a random number. Use the key to fill in some of the letters. Then use the hints to figure out the letters that are missing from the key.

Speech bubble (top):
13 10 9 9 5 ,
13 10 9 9 5 ,
13 10 9 9 5 ,
13 10 9 9 5 !

Speech bubble (right):
4 26 12 18 ,
13 2 21 10 24 12 13 2 6
4 20 10 2 3 15 2 25 12
23 10 12

Speech bubble (left):
20 5 2 25 12 18 24 1 -
19 2 20 12 18 2 24 .
19 2 9 9 5 8 25

hat are those sticks for?

Time to get ready for launch!

What do you think of my cool spaceship?

Speech bubble (bottom right):
18 12 25 5 26 12 5 15 !
12 13 18 25 8 5 20 9 6

HINTS

18 is either A or I.
12 is either G or T.
9 is either L or X.
25 is either S or Z.

KEY

1	2	3	4	5	6	7	8	9	10	11	12	13	14	15	16	17	18	19	20	21	22	23	24	25	26
K	B	O	D	Q	W				E	C		H	P	F	X	Z		M	R	V	J	Y			U

HEALTHY WORKOUT

FIND THESE OBJECTS IN THE SCENE.

baseball bat
button
candle
comb

doughnut
fish
fork
four-leaf clover

frying pan
golf club
ladder
loaf of bread

mallet
mitten
paper clip
pencil

pennant
ring
ruler
sailboat

slice of pizza
toothbrush

HINK PINKS

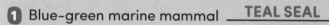

Hink Pinks are pairs of one-syllable words that rhyme. Each clue below can be answered by a Hink Pink. We've done the first one for you. Can you fill in the other Hink Pinks?

1 Blue-green marine mammal ___TEAL SEAL___

2 Bovine who loves to eat _____

3 Stinger's "Achoo!" _____

4 Adorable amphibian _____

Hinkie Pinkies are pairs of two-syllable words that rhyme. Can you fill in these Hinkie Pinkies? We've done the first one for you.

5 Iguana sorcerer ___LIZARD WIZARD___

6 Barnyard alarm clock who encourages others _____

7 Feathered friend who talks a lot _____

8 A small fake horse _____

Tic Tac Gnome

What do the garden gnomes in each row (horizontally, vertically, and diagonally) have in common?

what **trip** should **you take?**

Take this quiz to find out!

Do you like learning how things are made?

How

ADVENTUROUS are you?

that depends

what are you asking me to do **?**

MEH

I'm ready to try

SOMETHING NEW!

Actually I'd rather

STAY HOME

Never mind then. Grab your favorite book or movie and enjoy a

FUN NIGHT IN.

YOUR **DREAM DESSERT** is...

On a

CAMPING TRIP

you're the one who...

Brought an air mattress and favorite pillow

NO ONE SAID ADVENTURES HAD TO BE UNCOMFORTABLE!

snow Leopard

A mountain of ice cream

Packed the bare minimum. It's called

ROUGHING IT

for a reason!

CHOOSE ONE

Falcon

Friends describe you as

CAN'T GET ENOUGH

Which CLASS sounds more fun?

splatter painting 101

Introduction to Experiments

What's more YOUR STYLE?

The more COLORS the better!

Piles of candy

I'm NEUTRAL
I stick to one or two colors

CHILL

the LIFE of the PARTY

CANDY FACTORY TOUR

You love learning new things, and you also love eating sweets. Could a candy factory be any more perfect for you? We think not! Your sweet personality (see what we did there?) draws people to you, making it easy for you to make friends. And we'll bet those friends would appreciate some candy samples—just saying.

ICE PALACE EXPLORATION

Put on your parka and head off to the ice palaces. You prefer to chill out with friends and express yourself through your artsy side. Your laid-back, creative personality will thrive in these frosty masterpieces. Although you like exploring new things, you also love to be comfortable. We know you won't forget to keep warm with a cup of cocoa—or five.

THEME PARK ADVENTURE

Are you always on the lookout for the next exciting thing? Look no further, friend. It's here. Your thrill-seeking personality will have the time of its life spending the day riding roller coasters of all shapes and sizes. Your love for fun can be contagious, so be sure to invite friends along! Just don't eat any big meals before getting on the rides.

What did the glove say to the baseball?

"Catch you later!"

BEASTIE BASEBALL

BONUS! can you also find the ruler, comb, lollipop, and crayon?

tape dispenser

loaf of bread

bird

drinking straw

ladder

candle

peanut

saucepan

carrot

crown

slice of watermelon

slice of cake

sock

drumstick

saltshaker

domino

bell

take a RIDE

WHAT MADE THE DINOSAUR'S CAR STOP? To find out, read the road signs. The mile number on each sign tells you how many letters to count. The direction of the arrow tells you which direction to count the letters—right or left. The first three letters are done for you.

A F L __ __ __

__ __ __ __ -__ __ __ __ __ __ __ __ __ __ .

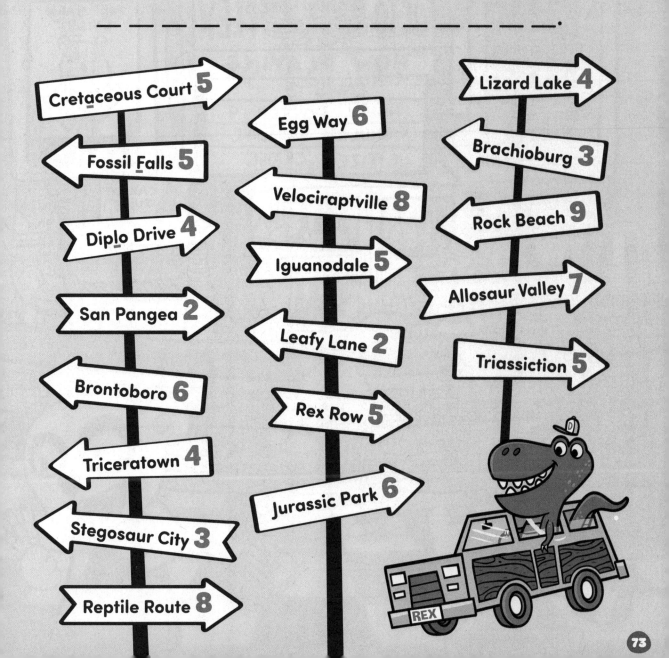

Cretaceous Court 5

Fossil Falls 5

Diplo Drive 4

San Pangea 2

Brontoboro 6

Triceratown 4

Stegosaur City 3

Reptile Route 8

Egg Way 6

Velociraptville 8

Iguanodale 5

Leafy Lane 2

Rex Row 5

Jurassic Park 6

Lizard Lake 4

Brachioburg 3

Rock Beach 9

Allosaur Valley 7

Triassiction 5

REX

SNACK COUNTER

Find 25 differences between the two pictures.

can you find these details in the picture below?

sudoku shades

Every pair of sunglasses should only appear once in each row, column, and 2 x 3 box. Fill in the squares by drawing or writing the name of each pair.

What do you call a potato wearing sunglasses?

A spec-tater

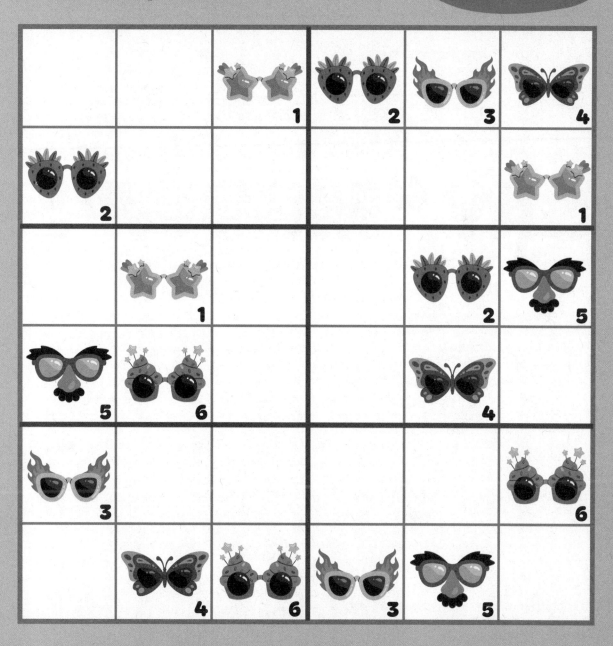

SAY "MEOW"!

Find 16 differences between the two pictures.

time to rhyme

Welcome to the Hillville Flea Market.
There's a star in a jar and a stork with a fork.
Can you find at least 15 other rhyming things?

PARTY DOGS

Four dogs brought different gifts to Chewie's birthday party. Using the clues, can you figure out what toy each dog brought and how Chewie thanked each one?

Put an **X** in every box that can't be true and an **O** in boxes that are true.

	the squeakiest chew toy ever	tennis balls to slobber on	a pre-chewed flying disc	the coolest treat dispenser	greeting card	email	phone call	high paw
Ruffus								
Barkley								
Woofgang								
chase								

CLUES

1 Chase enjoyed getting Chewie's email, which wasn't about the treat dispenser.

2 Ruffus spent time chewing on his gift before he wrapped it.

3 The dog who brought the tennis balls loved getting a greeting card to add to their collection.

4 Chewie called Barkley to thank him.

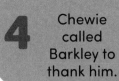

NACHO NIGHT

Can you figure out how many gallons of each topping the chef needs to make to fill all the orders?

guacamole
40 orders

1 gallon covers 10 orders

queso
40 orders

1 gallon covers 8 orders

sour cream
30 orders

1 gallon covers 7½ orders

salsa
30 orders

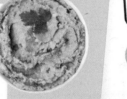

1 gallon covers 10 orders

brain breaks

THINK ABOUT IT

If you were an ASTRONAUT, what would you take with you to space?

If no SPACECRAFT had ever been sent into outer space, what things wouldn't we know?

If you were moving to MARS, what would you miss on EARTH?

start

STRETCH YOUR MATH SKILLS

Which planet is the dog going to visit? To find out, add the numbers on each planet you come to, and then take the path with the correct answer.

8 + 5

7 + 2

11

9

4 + 6

10

18

13

12

10

9 + 9

3 + 1

16

4

2

4 + 5

3 + 8

6 + 6

12

9

11

12

DO A WORD WORKOUT

Match the titles of these "Books Never Written" with their authors.

HINT: Try reading the authors' names out loud!

Did You See the Lights?

My Life in Outer Space

Weather in Space

Identify Constellations

Vera E. Cold

Leo O. Ryan

Aurora B. Ellias

I. Malone

BE LOGICAL

Which robot will get through the maze successfully by following its own program? Where are the instructions wrong for the other two?

exit

enter

KEY
E = Enter
L = Face left
R = Face right
F = Move forward 1 square
E = Exit

Alpha
ELFRFLFLFRFFE

Gamma
ELFRFLFRFRFFE

Beta
ELFRFLFFFRFFE

TICKLE YOUR FUNNY BONE

HA HA !!

ASTRONAUT #1: I'm going to the sun.
ASTRONAUT #2: You can't. It's too hot.
ASTRONAUT #1: Then I'll go at night.

what's wrong?

garden giggles

Which things in this picture are silly? It's up to you!

Race car Riddle

Each sentence will tell you where one letter is in the grid. Once you've found it, write it in the correct space below the riddle.

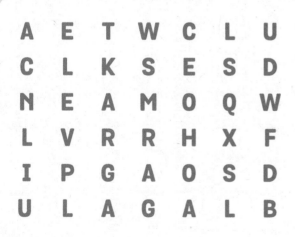

1. This letter is between a *G* and an *O*.
2. This letter is the first consonant in the top row.
3. Find this letter directly below the *Q*.
4. This letter appears in two of the four corners.
5. This letter is right above the letter *V*.
6. Find this letter in the center of the second row.
7. Look to the left of the *P* for this letter.
8. Look for this letter directly above the *B*.
9. Count two above the *M* for this letter.
10. Find this letter between two *O*s.

```
A E T W C L U
C L K S E S D
N E A M O Q W
L V R R H X F
I P G A O S D
U L A G A L B
```

why did the muffler stop before the finish line?

__ __   __ __ __   __ __ __ __ __ __ __ __ __ .
7 2 9 1 6 5 3 10 1 4 6 2 5 8

NOODLEDALE

FIND THESE OBJECTS IN THE SCENE.

anchor
baseball
cookie

crayon
crescent moon
flying saucer

harmonica
ice-cream cone
jump rope

peanut
pennant
saucepan

toothbrush
yo-yo

PB&J

Circle sets of three emojis together that have one peanut butter, one jelly, and one slice of bread. One side of each square must touch a side of another square in the same set. You are done when all the squares are circled.

Did you hear the joke about peanut butter and jelly?

I did, but I don't want to spread it.

our Annual Letter

_____ NOUN

This puzzle is best played with friends or family. Without letting them read the story, ask for the words or phrases under the blanks. (For example, the first thing you'll ask for is a *noun*.) After you've filled in all the blanks, read the story out loud.

Hello, friends and family!

Well, another year has gone by. It's been quite a(n) _____ for
NOUN

all of us. Our son, _____, invented a time machine and went
NAME

_____ years into the future. He came back with a new best
HIGH NUMBER

friend, a robot named _____-_____. He's very polite, even
NONSENSE WORD   NUMBER

though he eats the batteries in the TV remote. Our youngest, our

darling little _____, graduated from kindergarten and will
ANOTHER NAME

attend _____ in the fall. Our eldest, _____, and
COLLEGE NAME   ANOTHER NAME

her famous _____ got their own reality show!
HOUSEHOLD APPLIANCE

For our summer vacation, we went to _____, but
FAMOUS PLACE

unfortunately, Dad lost all his _____, and we had
ARTICLE OF CLOTHING (PLURAL)

to go back home. Speaking of Dad, he finally broke down and got the

kids a pet _____! On its first day in the house, it ate three
JUNGLE ANIMAL

_____ and 8,000 bowls of _____.
PIECE OF FURNITURE (PLURAL)   FOOD YOU DON'T LIKE

That about wraps it up. Happy _____, from our
PLURAL NOUN

_____ to yours!
NOUN

what's wrong?

on the wrong track

Which things in this picture are silly? It's up to you!

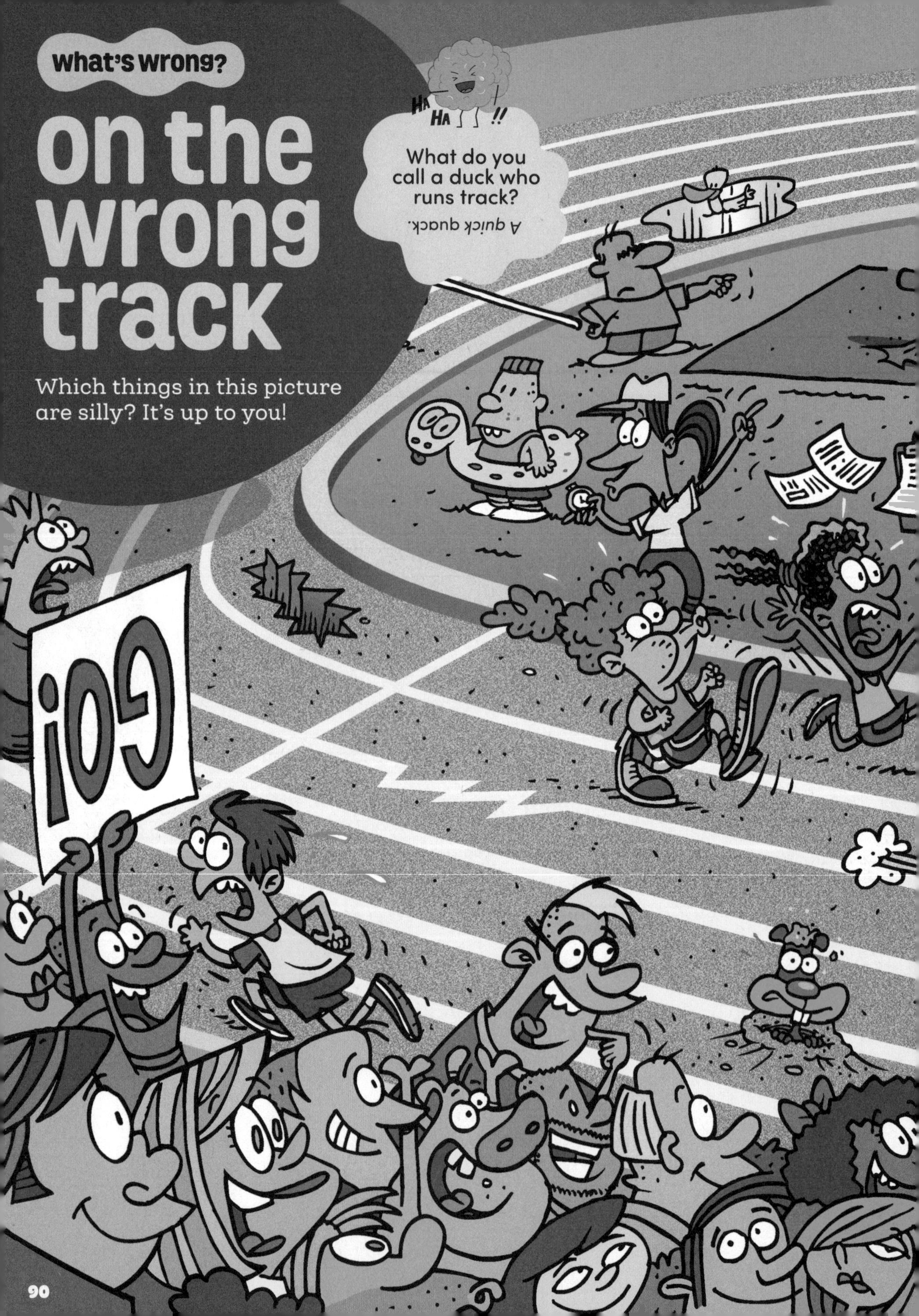

paper clip

key

present

butterfly

sock

button

mitten

baseball cap

flashlight

What kind of cheese do dogs like on their pizza?

Mutts-arella.

pup-peroni pizzas

guitar

clock

kayak

fried egg

shuttlecock

fork

early bird

Help the early bird catch the worm by using the clues to fill in the blanks. Each word is only one letter different from the word above it.

B I R D

1. To tie up
2. A musical group
3. A magician's stick
4. To wish for something
5. A small, hard lump on the skin
6. Not hot, but not cold

W O R M

I'm just winging it!

What on earth?

93

PIXIE PICNIC

Find 14 differences between the two pictures.

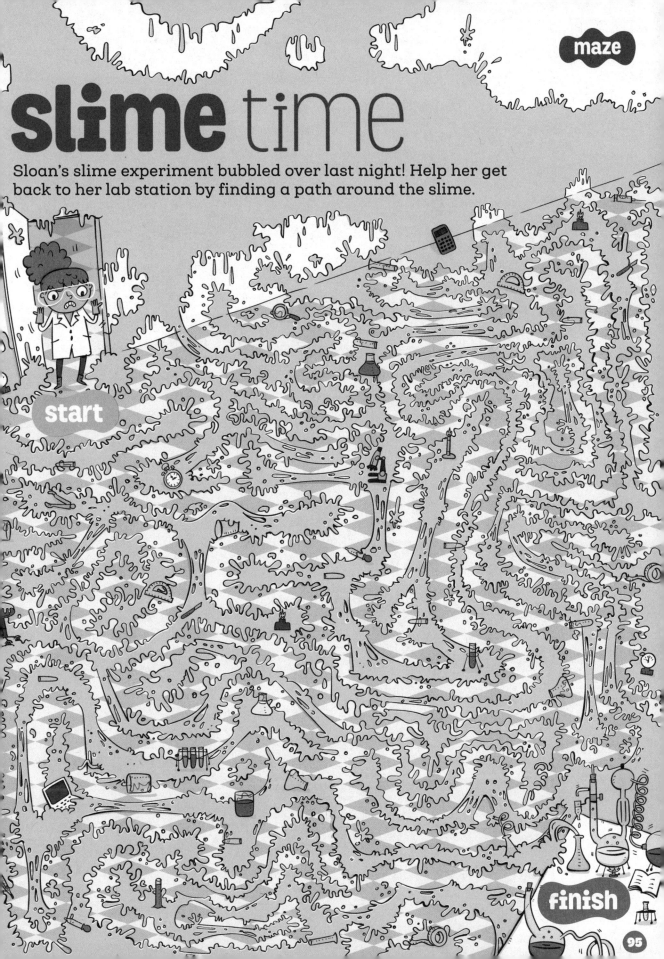

slime time

Sloan's slime experiment bubbled over last night! Help her get back to her lab station by finding a path around the slime.

maze

start

finish

95

panda-monium

Can you find the
polar bear? How
about the 12 dice?

SHAPE UP

Every shape should only appear once in each row, column, and 2 x 3 box. Fill in the squares by drawing or by writing the number of each picture.

Why didn't the square talk to the circle?

There was no point.

	1	2		3	4
		4		1	
2	5			4	6
3			1		
		3	6	5	
	6	5			2

PJ PARTY FUN

There are 10 words (not objects!) hidden in this scene. Can you find RED, ORANGE, YELLOW, GREEN, BLUE, PURPLE, PINK, BROWN, BLACK, and WHITE?

compound critters

Can you name the compound word that each picture represents?

Time for SCHOOL

These school supplies are getting ready to go back to school. Figure out what time they have specials on the first day and at what time.

Put an **X** in every box that can't be true and an **O** in boxes that are true.

	Library with Paige Turner	Phys Ed with Jim Nasium	Art with ROY G. BiV	Music with Zyla Phone	10:00 am	10:30 am	11:00 am	11:30 am
Penn Sill								
Mark Kerr								
Cal Q. Later								
Sharpay Nerr								

CLUES

1 Penn and Mark have Art and Music back-to-back.

2 Cal has to wait the longest for Library.

3 Sharpay has the earliest special, right before Penn's special.

4 Mark brought a clarinet for his special.

fishy subtraction

Solve each problem, and then fill in the blanks with the letter that corresponds to each number.

C
31
−25
___

T
11
−10
___

T
23
−19
___

E
15
−13
___

E
43
−34
___

I
27
−22
___

K
35
−28
___

S
47
−37
___

L
39
−31
___

N
19
−16
___

How many tickles does it take to make a jellyfish laugh?

___ ___ ___   ___ ___ ___ ___ ___ ___ ___
 1   2   3   4   5   6   7   8   9 10

brain breaks

THINK ABOUT IT

If you could have a pet DINOSAUR, which kind would you want? How would you train it?

What TWO QUESTIONS would you ask a dinosaur?

What COLOR do you think dinosaurs were?

TRAINASAURUS WRECKS

APATOSAURUS

BRACHIOSAURUS

WHINEDON

DO A WORD WORKOUT

ALLOSAURUS

IGUANODON

Five of these dinosaur names are real and five are made up. Which are fearsome and which are phony?

MEGALOSAURUS

TRICHERRYTOPS

IWANASAURUS

TETRAHEDRASAURUS

BE LOGICAL

Which of these shapes completes the baby dinosaur's eggshell?

A

B

C

D

TICKLE YOUR FUNNY BONE

HA HA !!

What do you call a dinosaur on a trampoline?

Tricera-hops.

STRETCH YOUR MATH SKILLS

Number the letters in the riddle question, left to right, from 1 to 26. Then solve the riddle by writing the corresponding letter in the blank spaces.

what dinosaur is a good sleeper?

A ___ ___ ___ ___ ___ - ___ ___ ___ ___ ___ ___ - ___ ___ .
3rd 9th 4th 22nd 16th 8th 14th 7th 18th 26th 23rd 11th 20th

what's wrong?

JUNGLE GYM

Which things in this picture are silly? It's up to you!

FINISH

104

beach day

Do some math, then get a laugh! Use the fractions of the words below to solve the riddles.

what's black and white and red all over?

_ _ _ _ _ _ _ _ _ _ _

_ _ _ _ _ _ .

Last ½ of PEAS
Middle ⅓ of LAUNCH
First ½ of BUSY
Last ⅔ of TURNED
Last ¼ of FUZZ
Middle ½ of DEBT
First ⅓ of RAISIN

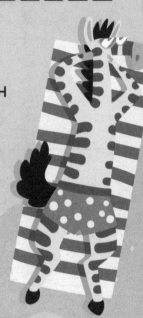

what do pigs put on their sunburn?

_ _ _ _ _ - _ _ _ _ _ .

Last ¾ of COIN
First ⅓ of KEY
Last ½ of HOME
Middle ⅓ of WINTER

what is the best day to go to the beach?

_ _ _ _ _ _ _ .

Middle ⅓ of RESULT
Last ½ of RIND
First ¼ of ACES
Middle ⅓ of RYE

FAST FOOD

FIND THESE OBJECTS IN THE SCENE.

banana
book
bottle
bowling ball

candy cane
candy corn
crescent moon
crown

eyeglasses
ghost
heart
hockey stick

ladder
leaf
macaroni
mitten

mug
necktie
pencil
screw

sock
spatula
wishbone
worm

107

Tic Tac Sharks

What do the snazzy sharks in each row
(horizontally, vertically, and diagonally) have in common?

JUiCY JOKES

Finish these fruit jokes by matching each riddle with its punch line.

1 What does a fruit say to apologize?

2 How many lemons grow on a lemon tree?

3 Why did the orange use sunblock?

4 Why was the apple feeling lonely?

5 Why did the strawberry call the grape for help?

6 What kind of fruit can fix your sink?

A All of them.

B It was in a jam.

C "I'm berry sorry."

D It was starting to peel.

E A plum-er.

F Because the banana split.

109

which dog in a wig are you?

Sometimes we're just a dog in a wig.
Which one are you?

1. WHICH OF THE FOLLOWING SOUNDS LIKE SOMETHING YOU WOULD WEAR REGULARLY?

A A funny graphic tee

B A pair of sweatpants

C Accessories to enhance your outfit

D Whatever is clean

2. WHICH IS EASIEST FOR YOU?

A Making your friends laugh

B Making sure everyone in your friend group feels included

C Putting together outfits that look great

D Trying new things

3. AT A BIRTHDAY PARTY, YOU USUALLY:

A Are in the middle of the crowd telling a funny story

B Love to support your friend, but are ready when it's time to go home

C Make sure to take lots of selfies with your friends

D Have fun doing whatever the rest of the group is doing

4. WHICH DREAM JOB SOUNDS BEST TO YOU?

A Stand-up comedian

B Author

C Actor

D Travel blogger

5. IN A SCHOOL PROJECT, YOU'RE THE ONE TO:

A Find all the funny photos for the presentation

B Do the research

C Volunteer to present in front of the class

D Take on whatever job the group needs done

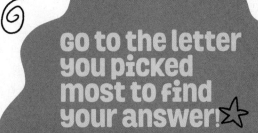

Go to the letter you picked most to find your answer!

A

YOU'RE KEVIN THE CLASS CLOWN

Whether it's telling a funny story or wearing a hilarious outfit, Kevin is ready to cheer up anyone's day. Like this jokester, you lighten the mood in a room with your positive attitude and constant supply of jokes.

B

YOU'RE CARRIE THE COZY HOMEBODY

Look for Carrie curled up on the couch with her favorite snack and a book! Like Carrie, you like what is predictable and are thoughtful when answering tough questions. You make others feel comfortable and confident in themselves!

C

YOU'RE GLORIA THE GLAMOROUS

Gloria is ready for her close-up with her perfectly styled hair and on-point fashion. Like Gloria, you're always ready to capture a moment, and you look great while doing it.

D

YOU'RE SCOTT THE FREE SPIRIT

Scott will try anything once, and his laid-back personality helps him fit in with any group. Like Scott's hair, you go with the flow. You like to try new things, and you pride yourself on your flexibility.

hidden pictures

fidget spinner

lime

crown

banana

needle

feather

slice of pizza

paper clip

spaceship

WOODLAND WHIMSY

slice of apple

magician's wand

ghost

sand dollar

seashell

knitted hat

mitten

lollipop

TOODLE-OO ZOO

Unscramble the animal names in these goodbyes to find each rhyming phrase.

What are the zoo's floors made of?

Reptiles.

HA HA !!

1. See you soon, big **NABBOO**.

_____

2. After awhile, **DOCCOREIL**.

_____

3. Got to go, **FABFULO**.

_____

4. Time to sleep, bighorn **PEESH**.

_____

5. Bye-bye, **FEBLUTTRY**.

_____

6. You're all that, **TIKTY TAC**.

_____

7. Take good care, **ZIRGLYZ EBAR**.

_____

8. That's all for me, **PENCHEZAMI**.

_____

9. Take a break, **TRANTELSAKE**.

_____

113

SPELUNKING SPLENDOR

...through the cave tunnels so they can add their signatures to the wall. Then add your own signature!

start

finish

VAL JACK GREG +
JAKE PATTI GRACE LIANN
ADEN marge HALLEY
BOB VANESSA
DOMIINGO
Barack ♥
maggie ⋛ judy
SHAW SETH leo BRUCE
NANCY

115

TOO MANY tacos

Can you find the burrito? How about the 12 peppers?

unicorn animals

Every animal should only appear once in each row, column, and 2 x 3 box. Fill in the squares by drawing or writing the number of each picture.

What do unicorns bring to party?

Their party horns.

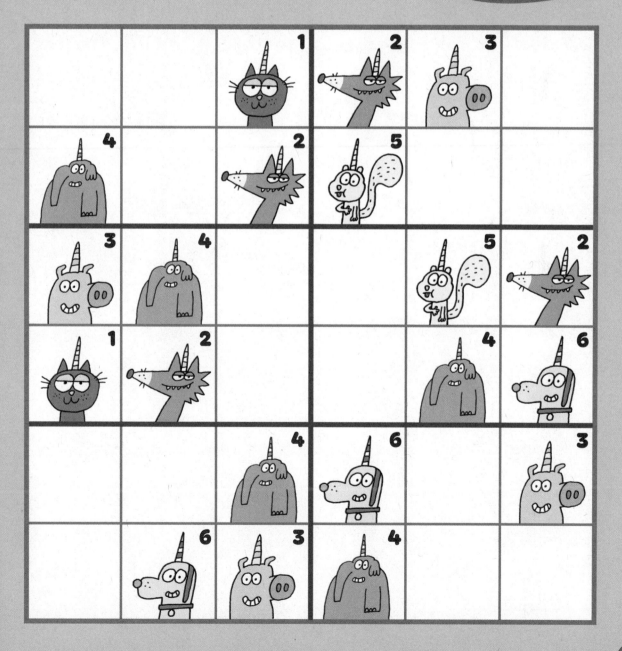

candy check

Can you find the 12 rubber ducks hidden in this photo?

no prob-llama

Each llama has an exact match except for one.
Can you find the one without a match?

Say this tongue twister three times fast!
Lately llamas love lazing.

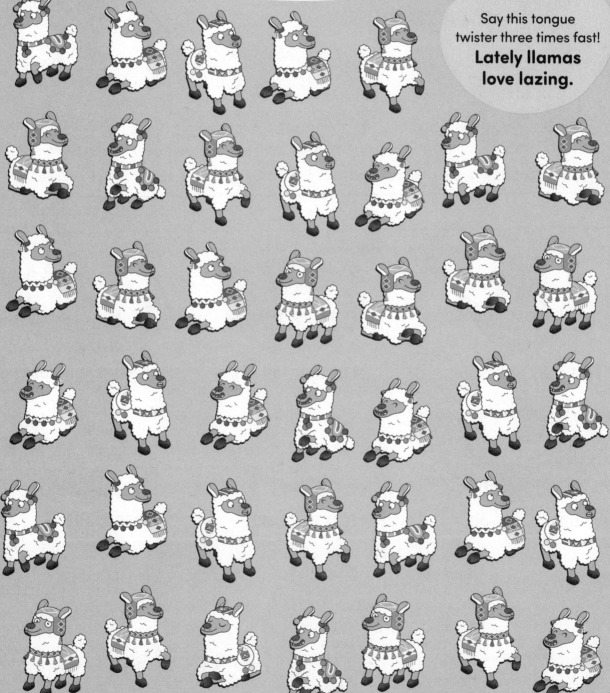

funny FLOATS

These floats took place in the annual "Pop Music Floatilla." Use the clues to figure out the order in which they were tied up.

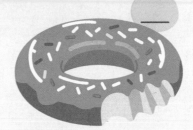

Floaty McDuckface

Doughnut Stop Me Now

Her Royal Pine-ness

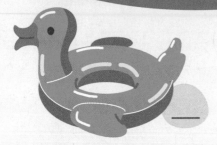

The Ripe Direction

Flamingo-go-GO

Keep Palm and Float On

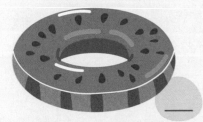

One in a Melon

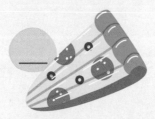

Pizza My Heart

Seas the Day

A. The fruit floats were not first or last.

B. Seas the Day was tied up between **Floaty McDuckface** and **Keep Palm and Float On.**

C. The 8th and 9th floats both have double letters in their names.

D. The 5th float was pink.

E. One of the animal floats took the first spot.

F. One in a Melon was tied up between **Her Royal Pine-ness** and **Flamingo-go-GO**.

READY, SET, SLOW

Each racer is taking a different path to the finish line, and each is moving at a different speed (in feet per hour). Can you figure out the order in which they will cross the finish line?

SPEEDY STR

44ft

11 fph

ACCELERATED AVE

30ft

6 fph

RAPID RD

7 fph

42ft

BRISK BLVD

24ft

8 fph

FINISH

BONUS!

Sloth is making a stew in his slow cooker for the post-race potluck. If he used a baker's dozen of twigs, two dozen shoots, and three dozen leaves, how many items did he use in all?

BE LOGICAL

Can you spot the column or row with five different shapes in it? Which column or row has five different colors in it?

	A	B	C	D	E
1					
2					
3					
4					
5					

LOL

TICKLE YOUR FUNNY BONE

What triangles are the coldest?

Ice-osceles triangles.

THINK ABOUT IT

If colors made noise, what do you think purple would sound like?

Which colors are your favorites to see together?

What color would you say your personality is?

DO A WORD WORKOUT

crimson
ruby
scarlet

amber
citron
canary

Which color does each group of three words describe?

azure
cobalt
teal

plum
mauve
lavender

sage
chartreuse
jade

PLAY WITH PATTERNS

Which set has the most squares containing circles? Which set has the fewest squares containing triangles?

what's wrong?

TRACK and field

Which things in this picture are silly? It's up to you!

crawly critters

To uncover the punch lines to these buggy jokes,
use the numbers under the blanks to find a
corresponding bug and letter.

what bug can tell time?

— — — — — — — — — — —
1   3   9   11   3   8   12   11   1   3   7

what kind of insect is bad at football?

— — — — — — — — — —.
1   5   14   10   2   9   4   2   4   4

which bug never does its chores?

— — — — — — — —
1   9   1   16   15   2   14   6

what do you call a musical insect?

— — — — — — —
1   7   14   10   2   14   6

125

SHARK-CUTERIE

FIND THESE OBJECTS IN THE SCENE.

adhesive bandage
balloon
baseball mitt
basketball
book

bottle
bug
car
dice
envelope

flashlight
hammer
heart
ladder
light bulb

lollipop
mug
moon
paintbrush
pencil
ring

shoe
sock
spatula
tiara
toothbrush
umbrella

127

Tic Tac Alien

What do the stellar aliens in each row
(horizontally, vertically, and diagonally) have in common?

your flight to _____

PLACE

This is best played with friends or family. Without letting them read the story, ask for the words or phrases under the blanks. (For example, the first thing you'll ask for is *a friend's first name*.) After you've filled in all the blanks, read the story out loud.

Welcome to _____ Airlines. We're sorry, but your flight has been delayed
FRIEND'S FIRST NAME

_____ hours, and your luggage just took off for _____. Also, we won't
BIG NUMBER   FARAWAY COUNTRY

be serving any food today, but all of our seat cushions are stuffed with _____. Our
FOOD YOU DON'T LIKE

onboard TVs aren't working, but the pilot will read from _____ during the flight over
YOUR FAVORITE BOOK

the plane's PA system.

We will begin boarding in _____ hours. If your socks have _____
BIG NUMBER   NOUN (PLURAL)

on them and your shoes are _____, you will board first. If your favorite song is
ADJECTIVE

_____, you can sit by a window. If that's not your favorite song, what's wrong with
YOUR FAVORITE SONG

you? Passengers with small children or extremely large _____ _____
COLOR   WILD ANIMAL (PLURAL)

should leave them in the cockpit with the pilot's babysitter. Oh! We do have some good news: Your

flight actually took off _____ minutes ago and will land on time!
SMALL NUMBER

what silly dinosaur are you?

Take this quiz to find out!

HOW DO YOU EXPRESS YOURSELF?

Actions

Words

WOULD YOU RATHER FOLLOW DIRECTIONS OR MAKE UP YOUR OWN?

WHEN YOU CLEAN YOUR ROOM, YOU PREFER TO LISTEN TO . . .

Music

Audiobooks or podcasts

WHICH DO YOU PREFER TO WATCH?

Shows adapted from books.

Reality shows

HOW DO YOU FEEL ABOUT BEING THE CENTER OF ATTENTION?

Please stop looking at me.

If it must happen, fine, but also, could it not?

I can't get enough!

Follow directions!

I consider rules more of "guidelines."

Whatever is quickest to grab.

I'm making my own creation.

velocichapter

"Just one more page," is Velocichapter's catchphrase. She has a sharp mind and loves to learn new things. She's often seen zipping from place to place with a book in hand, ready to devour her next story.

I like to help make plans!

WOULD YOU RATHER MAKE PLANS FOR YOUR FRIENDS OR HAVE YOUR FRIENDS MAKE THE PLANS?

I just want to show up and have fun.

Tricerachops

If you're hungry, you better hope Tricerachops is nearby. He is a wiz at whipping up creative meals, and he never forgets to add a little green garnish for pizzazz.

In a group! All my good ideas come when I work on a team.

Dinoscore

The real MVP! She is Dinoscore! She is the definition of a team player. Hogging the ball? She would NEVER! There might be an *I* in Dinoscore, but there definitely isn't one on Dinoscore's team!

SURPRISE! YOUR TEACHER JUST ASSIGNED A SCIENCE PROJECT. YOU CAN CHOOSE TO WORK ALONE OR IN A GROUP. WHICH DO YOU CHOOSE?

Alone, of course! I'll work so much quicker.

Tyrannosaurus Treks

Known for his love of the outdoors and fearless spirit, he's always looking for a new adventure and leaves no rock unturned—as long as his arms can reach the rocks, that is.

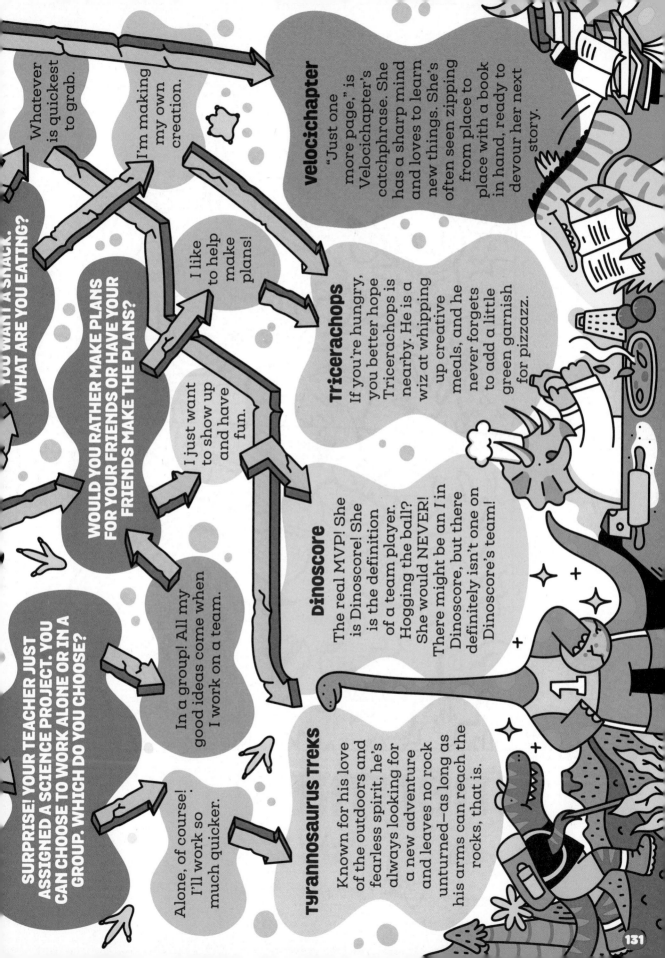

How did the mermaid get better at singing?

She practiced her scales.

ring

sock

baseball

banana

glove

pennant

golf club

wheel

baseball bat

mermaid music

teacup

party hat

slice of pizza

bow tie

wedge of lemon

comb

shuttlecock

dust pan

flashlight

box drop

To read the jumbled joke, move the letters from each column into the boxes directly above them, staying in the same row. But watch out: the letters do not always go in the boxes in the same order as they appear. Each letter is used only once. We've filled in some to get you started.

BONUS! Can you find 10 hidden carrots in the scene?

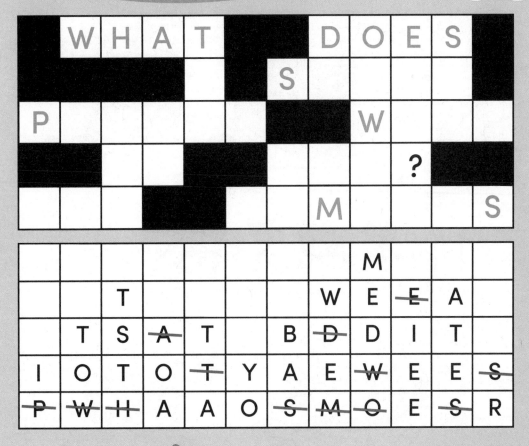

Grid (filled letters):
- Row 1: WHAT ... DOES
- Row 2: S ...
- Row 3: P ... W
- Row 4: ?
- Row 5: M ... S

Letter bank below:
- M
- T ... W E E̶ A
- T S A̶ T ... B D̶ D I T
- I O T O̶ T̶ Y A E W̶ W E E S̶
- P̶ W H̶ A A O S̶ M̶ O̶ E S̶ R

SKI TRIP

Find 15 differences between the two pictures.

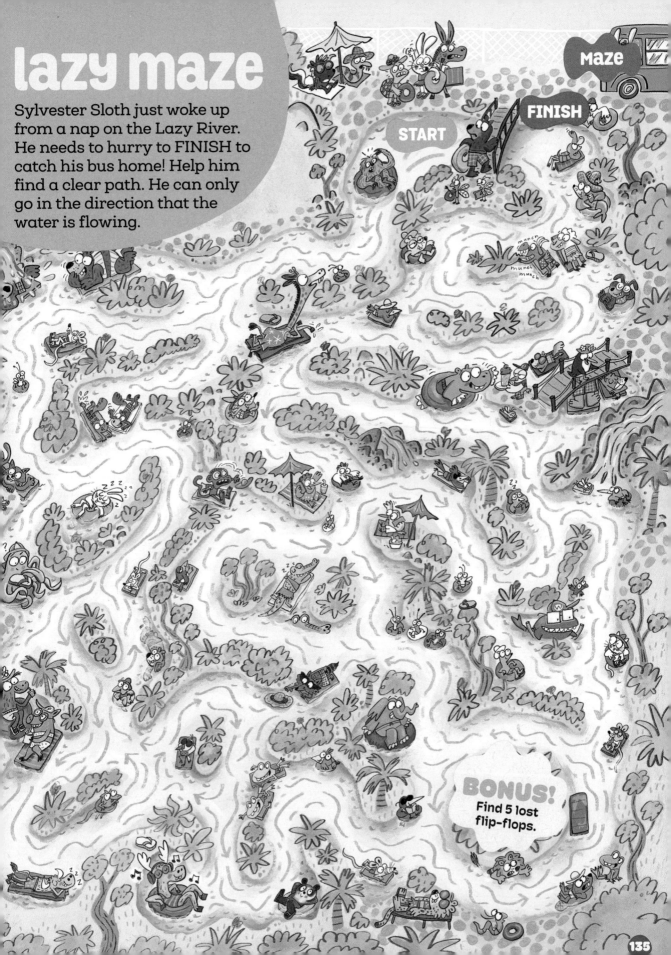

lazy maze

Sylvester Sloth just woke up from a nap on the Lazy River. He needs to hurry to FINISH to catch his bus home! Help him find a clear path. He can only go in the direction that the water is flowing.

MAZE

START

FINISH

BONUS! Find 5 lost flip-flops.

duck
duck swan

Can you find the
the swan? How about
the 12 frogs?

combo cuties

Every animal should only appear once in each row, column, and 2 x 3 box. Fill in the squares by drawing or writing the number of each picture.

What did the hairdresser say to the hot dog?

"Let's put you in a bun."

1		3	4		6
		6	1		
5	3			2	6
	4				1
		4	5	2	
2	5				3

CATNAPPING

Find 12 differences between the two photos.

fungi PARTY

Four mushroom friends are throwing a surprise party for their best friend. Using the clues, can you figure out which decoration and food each friend brought to the party?

	streamers	Balloons	Party Hats	candles	Black Forest cake	Fungus fudge	Petri Hotdish	Puffball-roni Pizza
Portia Bella								
shia Taki								
chantel Relle								
Matt sutaki								

Put an **X** in each box that can't be true and an **O** in boxes that are true.

CLUES

1 The friend who baked the cake brought the corresponding decoration.

2 Portia, the host, popped her hot dish in the oven right before Shia arrived with the balloons.

3 Chantel finally found party hats at the store next to the pizzeria.

4 Matt prefers baking to cooking.

GOt a minute?

To find the punch line, write each clock's letter in the space that has the matching digital time.

why was the clock so lonely?

I									
12:00	8:00	5:00	9:45	2:30	6:30	10:50	10:50	6:30	7:45

8:00	10:50	8:00	10:50	3:15	4:05	8:00	10:50

141

brain breaks

HINT: Take a ride!

TEST YOUR EYESIGHT

WHAT IS THIS?

Altitude or attitude?

Rudder or Shudder?

Crossword or Crosswind?

DO A WORD WORKOUT

Circle the real aviation term in each pair.

Sadstick or Joystick?

Flaperon or Flaperoff?

Headplane or Tailplane?

?!

THINK ABOUT IT

Describe where you live from an AIRPLANE'S POINT OF VIEW.

How is daydreaming like TRAVELING?

If you could travel anywhere, WHERE WOULD YOU GO? Why?

HA HA !!

Where do vans go swimming?

In a car pool.

BE LOGICAL

Twenty-two cars are driving on a road. The last eight cars stop for a traffic light. Three more cars turn onto the road from a store parking lot. One car pulls off the road with a flat tire, and another car pulls over to help. **How many cars are moving on the road?**

DECODE THE PUNCH LINE

Use the code to figure out the answer to the riddle.

what do boats do when they get sick?

E K G T O H D C

what's wrong?

happy birthday!

Which things in this picture are silly? It's up to you!

MATH MIRTH

Do some math, then get a laugh! Use the fractions of the words listed under the blanks to solve the three riddles.

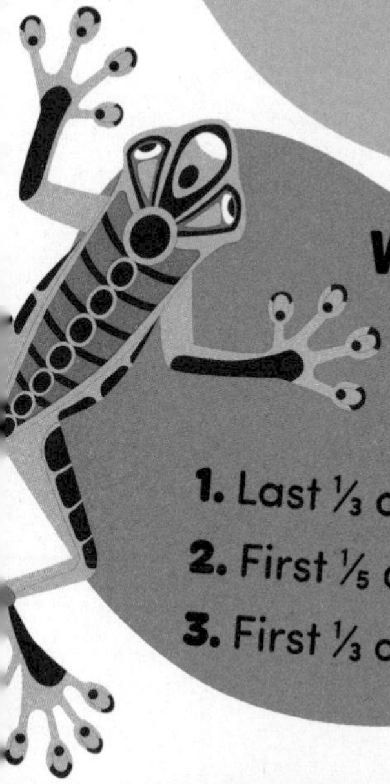

what do you call a FROG caught in the mud?

U _ _ _ _ _ _ _.

1. Last ⅓ of **YOU**
2. First ⅕ of **NEVER**
3. First ⅓ of **HOT**
4. Last ½ of **STOP**
5. Last ½ of **COPY**

what is a snake's favorite school subject?

_ _ _ _ _ – _ _ _ _ _ _.

1. First ½ of **HILL**
2. Last ⅖ of **CLASS**
3. First ½ of **TOOK**
4. Last ⅓ of **MEMORY**

what do you call a RICH lizard?

_ _ _ _ _ _ _ _ – _ _ _ _ _.

1. First ⅗ of **CHALK**
2. First ¾ of **MELT**
3. Last ¾ of **NEON**
4. First ⅔ of **AIM**
5. Last ½ of **MORE**

ALARM ANTICS

FIND THESE OBJECTS IN THE SCENE.

artist's brush
bell
canoe
crayon
crescent moon

drinking straw
drumstick
envelope
feather
flashlight

glove
hammer
hat
hockey stick
ice-cream cone

ice pop
inner tube
ladder
ladle
leaf

lollipop
mitten
mug
needle

pencil
ruler
slice of pie
slice of pizza

spatula
tack
toothbrush
waffle

CLICK!

Zzz

147

Tic Tac Axolotl

What do the silly axolotls in each row
(horizontally, vertically, and diagonally) have in common?

Lotl Letters

This axolotl got the letters in his notes mixed up! Circle
every other letter to find which note he meant to write
to his friend and which one goes on his grocery list.

IGLEOTVSENYAOXUOALLOOTTLLS

monster Match

Finish these monster jokes by matching each riddle with its punch line.

1. Which monster likes to dance?

2. What should you do if a monster rolls his eyes at you?

3. What do monsters ride at the amusement park?

4. How does a monster count to 23?

5. Why didn't the monster finish her homework?

A On its fingers.

B The boogie man.

C The scary-go-round.

D She wasn't that hungry.

E "Hello, hello, hello!"

F Roll them back to him.

6. How do you greet a three-headed monster?

PLAY DAY!

The park is a busy place today! There are at least 18 items in this scene with silly rhyming names, like swift gift, snake cake, and flower power. Can you find them all?

Where can a burger get a good night's sleep?

On a bed of lettuce.

coin

cell phone

triangle ruler

acorn

hammer

arrow

baseball bat

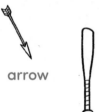
boomerang

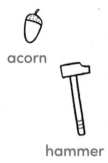
lizard

POWER

burger vs. fries

chick

mug

pencil

fish

caterpillar

comb

crown

letter drop

Only 8 of the letters in the top line will work their way through this maze to land in the numbered squares at the bottom. When they get there, they will spell out the answer to the riddle.

BONUS!
Each cat in the pile has a match except one. Can you find the one without a match?

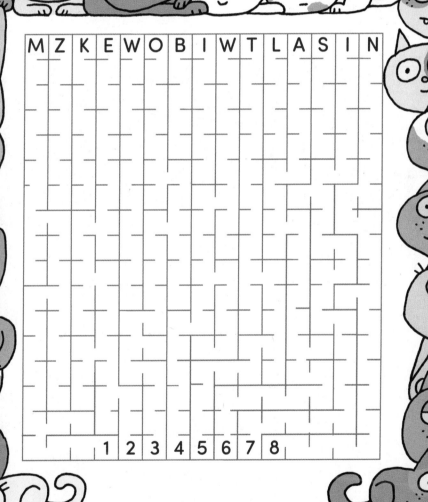

M Z K E W O B I W T L A S I N

1 2 3 4 5 6 7 8

what do you call a pile of cats?

A _ _ _ _ _ - _ _ _ _ .

153

MERMAID MAZE

The sun is out and Maida wants to catch some rays! Can you help her find a path to her favorite sunbathing rock?

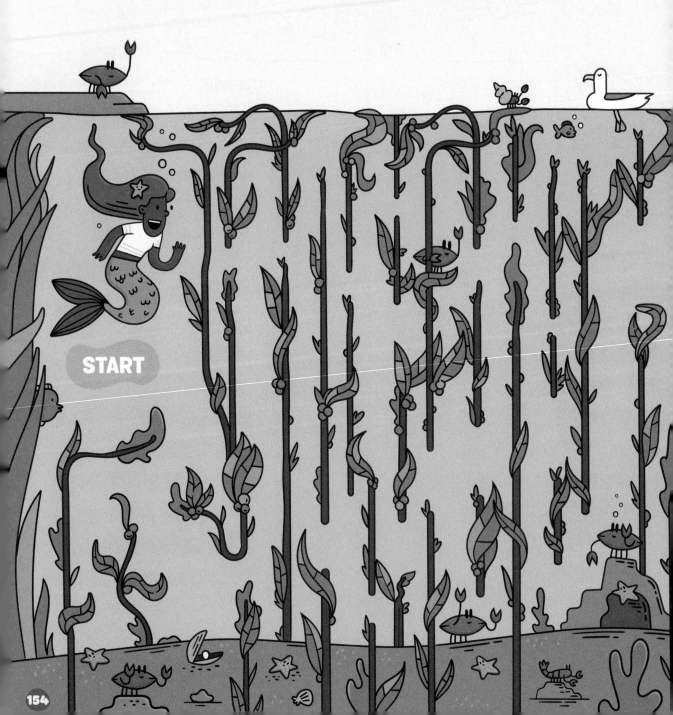

START

spot the impostor

doughnut dash

Can you find the cupcake? How about the 12 strawberries?

FINISH

156

yoga moves

Every yoga animal should only appear once in each row, column, and 2 x 3 box. Fill in the squares by drawing or writing the number of each picture.

Which band plays music that makes you want to stretch?

A rubber band.

1	2				3
4			5		1
	4	1	2	5	
	5	6	3	1	
6		2			5
5				6	2

happy **feet**

This highland cow loves her mismatched socks! Circle sets of four socks together that have one of each silly sock. One side of each square must touch a side of another square in the same set of four. You are done when all the squares are circled.

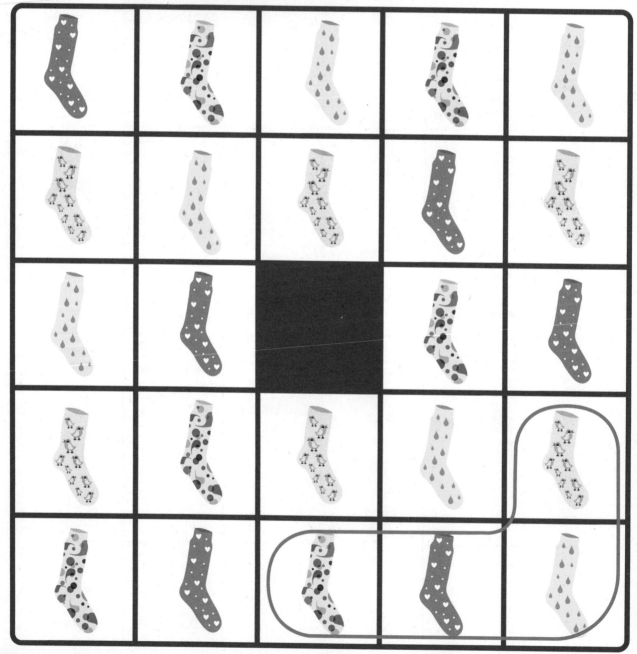

commander cactus

Can you figure out the order in which these scenes occurred? HINT: Start with E.

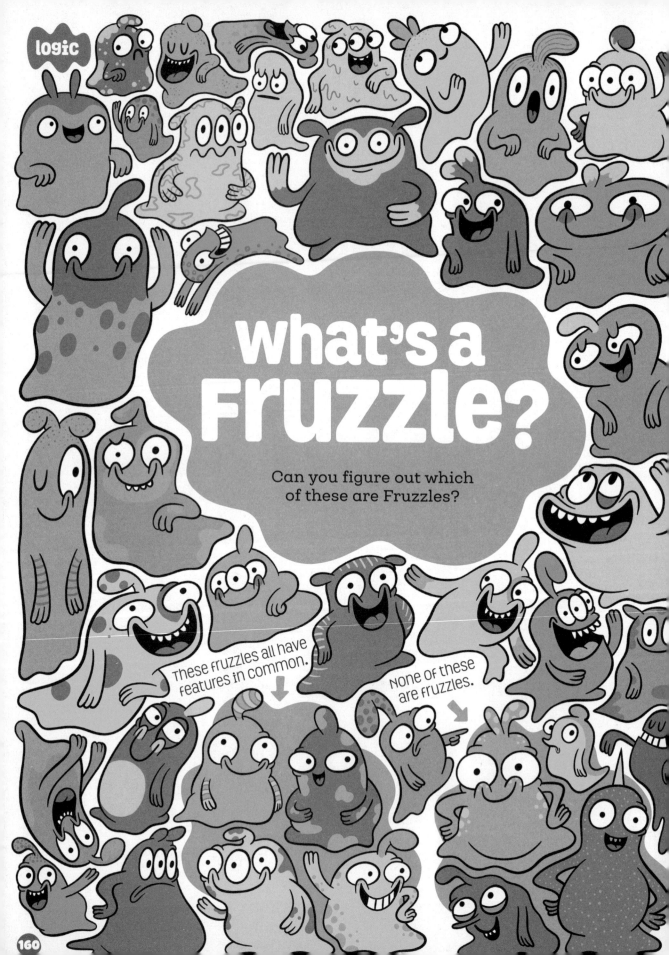

what's a Fruzzle?

Can you figure out which of these are Fruzzles?

These fruzzles all have features in common.

None of these are fruzzles.

GOING BANANAS

Find the first number along the orange row, and the second number along the blue column. Then find the banana where those two numbers meet. Write the letters you find in the blanks.

BONUS! Using the same code, write your own puzzle for this joke: Why was the banana so popular? IT HAD APPEAL.

10	A	N	W	O	V	B	P	S	S	J	T
9	X	Q	D	N	E	C	L	N	A	C	P
8	U	K	P	X	D	D	I	I	B	A	L
7	L	E	D	C	G	Q	S	H	O	P	Z
6	Q	W	C	D	A	R	V	A	H	Y	Q
5	T	A	N	U	F	A	A	K	M	R	B
4	V	O	N	R	R	N	G	X	O	S	C
3	C	B	V	K	H	P	G	R	P	W	E
2	Y	E	N	O	S	L	T	E	Q	E	F
1	R	U	T	H	Z	E	I	E	X	Y	L
	1	2	3	4	5	6	7	8	9	10	11

why don't bananas get lonely?

T __ __ __ __ __ __ __ __ __ __ __ __ __ __ __
3,1 9,6 8,1 1,2   6,5 7,9 2,6 6,5 1,2 5,2   9,6 6,5 3,5 7,3

__ __ __ __ __ __ __ __ __ __ __ __ __ __ __ .
6,5 4,4 9,4 1,8 3,5 3,9   8,8 3,5   11,5 1,8   3,5 4,7 9,6 8,1 5,2

brain breaks

BE LOGICAL

Use the clues to figure out which shirt belongs to each player.

HINT: try reading the names out loud!

Shirts: NETT · BALL · THYME · YUSS · LEE · KING · DEWITT · MELL · THON

JUSTIN is never late for practice.

JEAN makes super-smart plays on the field.

BROCK eats green vegetables to fuel up.

CLARA plays a woodwind instrument to relax before games.

JOE loves making his teammates laugh.

CRYSTAL is good at predicting who will win.

MARY never tires on the field.

KARA brings after-game treats for the team.

AL likes to volunteer to help the coach.

LOL

TICKLE YOUR FUNNY BONE

What is a waiter's favorite sport?

Tennis, because they serve so well.

TEST YOUR EYESIGHT

WHAT IS THIS?

HINT: The name includes a bumpy, green food.

THINK ABOUT IT

What makes you enjoy a SPORT?

Name as many sports as you can in which players HIT A BALL.

How is your family like a sports team?

DO A WORD WORKOUT

Change one letter in each word to spell a piece of sports equipment.

grove

hall

new

clues

states

bot

pleats

rocket

boggles

STRETCH YOUR MATH SKILLS

Can you figure out how many total runs were scored in the two games?

In baseball action today, the Seagulls scored 9 runs to beat the Pelicans by 3. Meanwhile, the Seals defeated the Loggerheads by scoring 5 fewer runs than the Pelicans.

What did the vegetable say to start the party?

Lettuce turnip the beet!

PRODUCE PARTY

BONUS!
can you
also find
the mouse,
shoe, and
candle?

button

kite

fork

drinking
straw

ladle

lightning bolt

pennant

umbrella

artist's brush

tack

crescent
moon

heart

ruler

Have an ICE Day!

Circle the words or phrases containing *ICE* hidden in the grid. The word *ICE* has been replaced with a .
Look down, across, and diagonally.

"Ice" to meet you!

```
W O E W J U S T 🧊 E N T
S F T C H O 🧊 H E R E Y
E F M 🧊 B E R G E S T E
R 🧊 A O R 🧊 S K A T E D
V S G N P A I R O F D 🧊
🧊 L N T 🧊 A S Y T O D 🧊
A 🧊 I H Y P W O V E A P
🧊 O F I R E O G L O O A
F F 🧊 N I N G P B S 🧊 C
I P N 🧊 🧊 C U B E O T K
S I T W L I 🧊 B O X N 🧊
H E G B R E A K T H E 🧊
```

WORDS

~~ICEBERG~~
OFFICE
SOLSTICE
CHOICE
ICEBOX
JUSTICE
SERVICE
ICE SKATE
VOICE
MAGNIFICENT
PAIR OF DICE
ICE CUBE
SLICE OF PIE
BREAK THE ICE
ICE POP
ON THIN ICE
ICE PACK
ICE FISH

BONUS!

Put the uncircled letters in order on the blank spaces below to finish the joke.

A police officer stopped a person who was driving with two penguins in the back seat. The police officer said, "Why don't you take those penguins to the zoo?" The person replied,

"_ _ _ _ _ _ _ _ _ _ _ _

_ _ _ _ _ _ _ _ _ _ _. _ _ _ _ _ _

_ _ _ _ _ _ _ _ _ _ _ _ _ _ _!"

LAUGH ATTACK

A wonderfully weird board game for four to six players.

YOU WILL NEED:

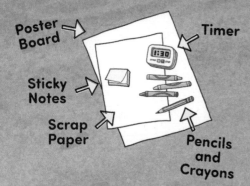

Poster Board

Timer

Sticky Notes

Scrap Paper

Pencils and Crayons

TO PLAY:

1 Cut out seven rectangles from poster board to use as game cards. Color one side of each card: two yellow cards, two blue cards, two green cards, and one red card.

2 Each player draws a silly character on a small sticky note to use as a game piece. The player with the next birthday goes first and becomes the scorekeeper.

3 Shuffle the cards. Have another player hold them out (color-side down) for you. Pick one, and go to the next unplayed space of that color. If you go to a space that's:
BLUE OR YELLOW: All other players compete in the challenge. Set a timer for one minute and 30 seconds for players to draw or write. Close your eyes while answers are turned in. Choose one at random. That person gets two points. Enjoy sharing all the answers!

RED: Do the action written on the space. Lose a point (if you have any).

GREEN: Act out the scenario to earn a bonus point.

4 The scorekeeper writes down any points earned. The player to your left picks a card next.

5 If there are no unplayed spaces left in the color you pick, go to Finish. The first player to do so earns five points. After you reach Finish, you may continue to compete in challenges and earn points, but skip your turn to choose a card. Once all players reach the finish, the player with the most points wins!

START HERE.

START

DRAW
A self-portrait (Draw with your eyes closed.)

ACT OUT
A goat stepping on a Lego

WRITE
A caption for this cartoon

OH NO!
You're a pterodactyl now. Let out a screech.

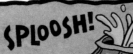

SPLOOSH!

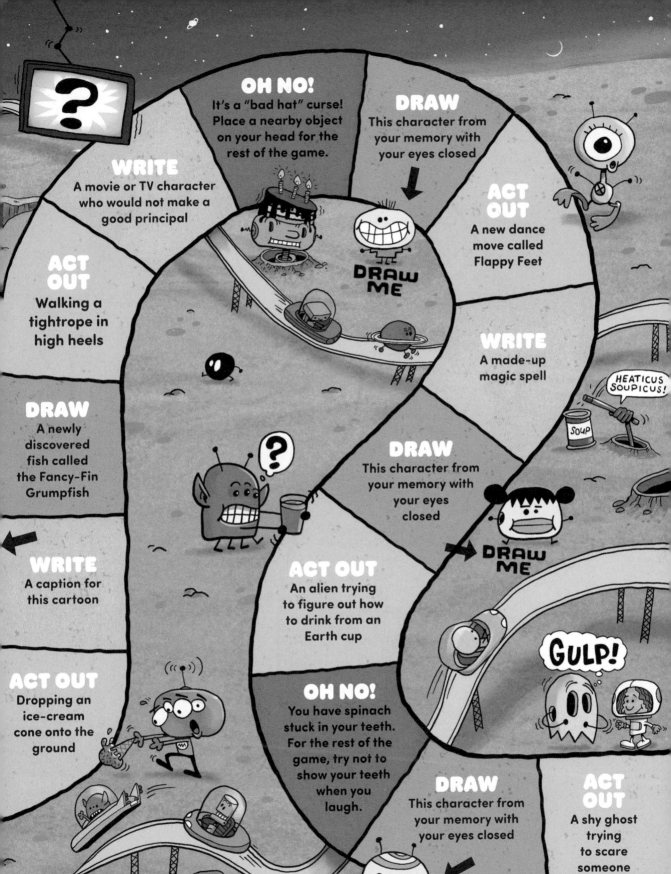

?

WRITE
A movie or TV character who would not make a good principal

OH NO!
It's a "bad hat" curse! Place a nearby object on your head for the rest of the game.

DRAW
This character from your memory with your eyes closed

ACT OUT
A new dance move called Flappy Feet

ACT OUT
Walking a tightrope in high heels

DRAW ME

WRITE
A made-up magic spell

HEATICUS SOUPICUS!

SOUP

DRAW
A newly discovered fish called the Fancy-Fin Grumpfish

DRAW
This character from your memory with your eyes closed

DRAW ME

WRITE
A caption for this cartoon

ACT OUT
An alien trying to figure out how to drink from an Earth cup

GULP!

ACT OUT
Dropping an ice-cream cone onto the ground

OH NO!
You have spinach stuck in your teeth. For the rest of the game, try not to show your teeth when you laugh.

DRAW
This character from your memory with your eyes closed

ACT OUT
A shy ghost trying to scare someone

DRAW ME

(Continued on next page)

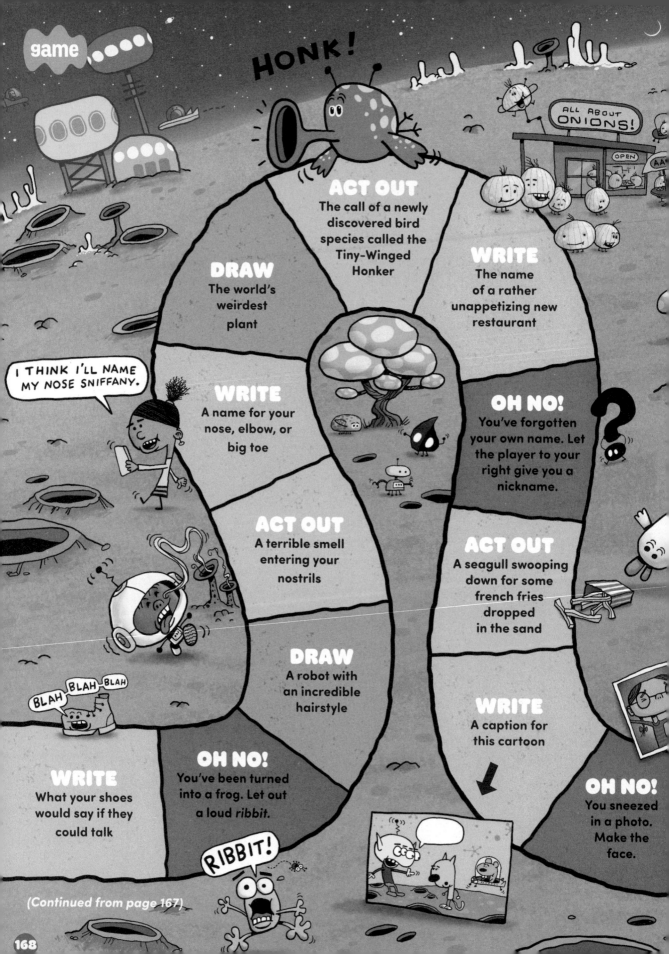

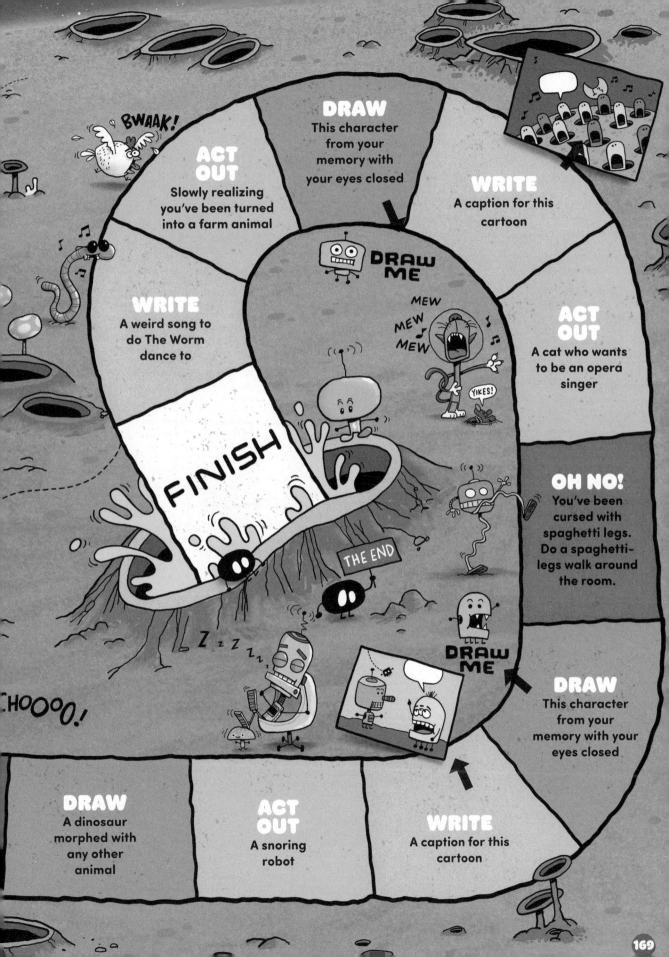

DRAW This character from your memory with your eyes closed

ACT OUT Slowly realizing you've been turned into a farm animal

WRITE A caption for this cartoon

WRITE A weird song to do The Worm dance to

DRAW ME

ACT OUT A cat who wants to be an opera singer

FINISH

OH NO! You've been cursed with spaghetti legs. Do a spaghetti-legs walk around the room.

THE END

DRAW ME

DRAW This character from your memory with your eyes closed

DRAW A dinosaur morphed with any other animal

ACT OUT A snoring robot

WRITE A caption for this cartoon

what's wrong?
ball game GIGGLES

Which things in this picture are silly? It's up to you!

FRONT COVER

BRAIN BREAKS
pages 2-3

BE LOGICAL:

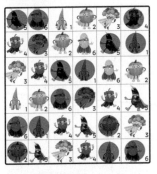

DO A WORD WORKOUT: 1. false **2.** true
3. false **4.** true **5.** false
TEST YOUR EYESIGHT: an orange slice

A GROUP OF . . . page 5
WHAT DO YOU GET WHEN TWO GIRAFFES COLLIDE? A GIR-AFFIC JAM.

PIRATE PLUNGE pages 6-7

YOU'VE GOT TO BE KITTEN ME! page 9

1. E **2.** C **3.** B **4.** A **5.** D **6.** F

DINO DIVERS page 12

LAUGHTER AROUND THE WORLD page 13

ON THE WAY GNOME pages 14-15

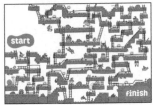

There are more ants than flowers.

CRAB CRAZE page 16

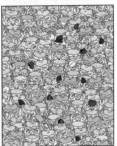

FACE-OFF page 17

JUST DUCKIES
pages 18-19

TALENT SHOW
page 20

BLOBERT: slime juggling; 1st
ESHRIEKIEL: guitar solo; 2nd
FIREGUS: interpretive dance; honorable mention
GOOPSON: self-portrait; 3rd

GET COORDINATED
page 21

WHAT DID THE STUDENT SAY TO THE CALCULATOR? "I AM COUNTING ON YOU."

BRAIN BREAKS
pages 22-23

TEST YOUR EYESIGHT: a microphone
DO A WORD WORKOUT: gaggle, zigzag, gauge, luggage, gadget
STRETCH YOUR MATH SKILLS: Nylah and Rodrigo each made five hits. Kiernan made seven hits, and Elianna made nine.
BE LOGICAL:

WHOOO'S THERE?
page 25

1.KNOCK, KNOCK.
WHO'S THERE?
WHO.
WHO WHO?
I DIDN'T KNOW YOU SPOKE OWL!
2. KNOCK, KNOCK.
WHO'S THERE?
OWL.
OWL WHO?
OWL NIGHT LONG I WAS AWAKE!

POP THE BALLOON
pages 26-27

TIC TAC CAT page 28

space doodles polka-dot background teal cat	polka-dot background two-color background	polka-dot background looking down bow ties
space doodles sunglasses	sunglasses teal cat bow ties two-color background	looking down sunglasses
space doodles doughnut doodles bow ties	two-color background doughnut doodles	looking down teal cat doughnut doodles

CAT WALK:
Here are the words we found. You may have found others. TYPE, PEA, PEACH, EACH, CHIN, HINT, IN, INTO, TO, TOP, PLOT, LOT, OTHER, THE, THERE, HE, HERE, REAL, ALSO, SO, SOME, ME, MEAT, EAT, AT, TUNA.

answers

UNIDENTIFIED UFOs
page 31

1. E **2.** H **3.** J **4.** G **5.** B **6.** A **7.** I **8.** C
9. F **10.** D

FUN AND GAMES
page 32

ZZzzzzZZzzzz
page 33

1. CRIB **4.** BLANKET **10.** TUB **12.** BEDROOM
18. MOON **21.** NIGHT OWL **28.** LULLABY
34. YAWN **37.** NIGHTMARE **45.** EYES
48. SHEEP **52.** PILLOW **57.** WAKE UP
62. PAJAMAS **68.** SLIPPERS **75.** STARS
79. SLEEPING BAG **89.** GOOD
92. DREAMING

PASS THE POPCORN
page 34

LADDER UP
page 35

answers

HEAPS OF SHEEP

page 36

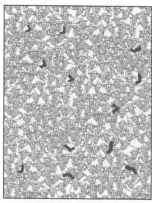

A-DOUGH-RABLE DOUGHNUTS page 37

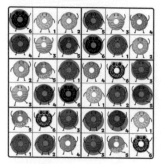

SHADOW MATCH

page 38

SNAILS ON THE GO!

page 39

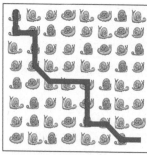

Here is one path we found. You may have found others.

FAN-CACTUS DESTINATIONS

page 40

SPIKE: skiing in Switzerland; January
FLORA: kayaking in Antarctica; March
CARL: ice-skating in Canada; December
FLUFFY: glacier hiking in Iceland; February

PLAYING PATTERNS

page 41

PLAYER 1
A. 16 [adds one more (+2, +3, +4, +5)]
B. 0 [subtract increments of 2 (-2, -4, -6)]
C. 40 (double the preceding number)
D. 1 (divide each by 3)
E. 3 (divide each by 2)
F. 625 (multiply each by 5)
G. 13 (add 4, then subtract 2)
H. 256 (multiply each number by itself)
I. 24 (divide by 3, then multiply by 6)
J. 4 (multiply by 2, then divide by 10)
TOTAL SCORE: 982

PLAYER 2
A. 32 (double the preceding number)
B. 26 [add sequence of even numbers (+4, +6, +8)]
C. 15 [subtract increments of 5 (-10, -15, -20)]
D. 6 (divide each by 10)
E. 400 (double the preceding number)
F. 15 (divide each by 2)
G. 16 (add 4, then subtract 8)
H. 120 (divide by 3, then multiply by 6)
I. 144 (multiply by 2, then add 4)
J. 18 (add 6, then subtract 3)
TOTAL SCORE: 792

BRAIN BREAKS

pages 42-43

STRETCH YOUR MATH SKILLS: A
TEST YOUR EYESIGHT: sequins on a mermaid costume
DO A WORD WORKOUT: 1. final or last, **2.** stain, **3.** cast, **4.** snail, **5.** tint
BE LOGICAL: Moonbeam visited her grandparents on March 12.

PENGUIN POOL PARTY page 45

WHERE DO PENGUINS LIKE TO GO SWIMMING? THE SOUTH POOL.

FANCY FLAMINGOS

pages 46-47

TIC TAC TACO page 48

Sour cream Lettuce on top Chili pepper	Tomatoes on bottom Lettuce on top	Tomatoes in middle Lettuce on top Olive
Sour cream Meat on top	Tomatoes on bottom Meat on top Olive Chili pepper	Tomatoes in middle Meat on top
Sour cream Cheese on top Olive	Tomatoes on bottom Cheese on top	Tomatoes in middle Cheese on top Chili pepper

12 DAYS OF CUTENESS pages 50-51

PURR-ITO AND FRIENDS page 52

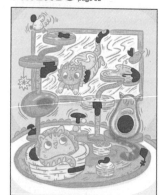

ROAD TRIP CROSS-OUT

page 53

WHAT DO YOU GET IF YOU CROSS A BIRD, A CAR, AND A DOG? A FLYING CARPET.

SOCK SEARCH page 54

PRETZEL PATH

page 55

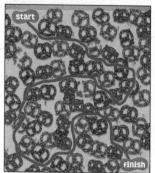

WHICH WALRUS?

page 56

SOUND EFFECTS

page 57

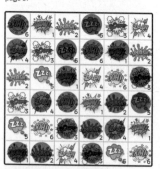

BEST FRIENDS FUR-EVER pages 58-59

WHAT'S A GIBBLE?

page 60

Gibbles have two antennae, two triangles, and one rectangle on their bodies.

ANIMAL ADDITION

page 61

11 + 22 = 33
35 + 21 = 56
47 + 12 = 59

BRAIN BREAKS

pages 62–63

TEST YOUR EYESIGHT: a butterfly wing
DO A WORD WORKOUT: 1. false **2.** true
3. false **4.** false **5.** true
BE LOGICAL:

COSMIC CODE page 65

HELLO, HELLO, HELLO, HELLO!
BUT I HAVEN'T HAD BREAKFAST YET.
ROASTING MARTIAN-MALLOWS.
IT'S OUT OF THIS WORLD!

HEALTHY WORKOUT pages 66–67

HINK PINKS page 68

1. TEAL SEAL **2.** CHOW COW **3.** BEE'S SNEEZE **4.** CUTE NEWT **5.** LIZARD WIZARD **6.** ROOSTER BOOSTER **7.** WORDY BIRDY **8.** PHONY PONY

TIC TAC GNOME page 69

bird watering can shovel	bird hand on hip	bird polka-dot hat white hair and beard
watering can rosebush	shovel rosebush white hair and beard hand on hip	polka-dot hat rosebush
overalls watering can white hair and beard	overalls hand on hip	overalls polka-dot hat shovel

BEASTIE BASEBALL

page 72

TAKE A RIDE page 73

WHAT MADE THE DINOSAUR'S BIKE STOP? A FLAT TIRE-ANNOSAURUS.

SNACK COUNTER

pages 74–75

PILE OF PUPS page 76

SUDOKU SHADES

page 77

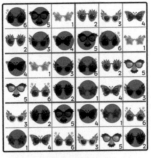

SAY "MEOW"! page 78

TIME TO RHYME

page 79

We found these rhymes. You may have found others! bent/tent, pug/rug, squirrel/pearl, lizard/wizard, llamas/pajamas, goat/coat, sheep/jeep, doll/shawl, stamp/lamp, Great Dane/train/plane, fish/dish, duck/puck, wombat/flat/hat, cat/bat, mouse/blouse, frog/log, star/jar, kittens/mittens, bear/chair, cricket/ticket, jacket/racket, stork/fork, raccoon/balloon, baboon/bassoon, chick/pogo stick, fox/socks.

PARTY DOGS page 80

RUFFUS: a pre-chewed flying disc; high paw
BARKLEY: the coolest treat dispenser; phone call
WOOFGANG: tennis balls to slobber on; greeting card
CHASE: the squeakiest chew toy ever; email

NACHO NIGHT page 81

SOUR CREAM: 4 gallons
GUACAMOLE: 4 gallons
SALSA: 3 gallons
QUESO: 5 gallons

BRAIN BREAKS

pages 82–83

STRETCH YOUR MATH SKILLS:

DO A WORD WORKOUT: DID YOU SEE THE LIGHTS? by Aurora B. Ellias; **MY LIFE IN OUTER SPACE** by I. Malone; **WEATHER IN SPACE** by Vera E. Cold; **IDENTIFY CONSTELLATIONS** by Leo O. Ryan
BE LOGICAL: Gamma will make it through the maze. The instructions for both Alpha and Beta went wrong after the third F.

RACE CAR RIDDLE

page 85

WHY DID THE MUFFLER STOP BEFORE THE FINISH LINE? IT WAS EXHAUSTED.

NOODLEDALE

pages 86–87

PB&J

page 88

PUP-PERONI PIZZAS

page 92

EARLY BIRD page 93

1. BIND **2.** BAND **3.** WAND **4.** WANT **5.** WART **6.** WARM

PIXIE PICNIC page 94

answers

SLIME TIME page 95

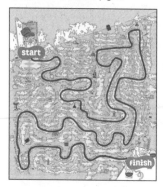

PANDA-MONIUM

page 96

SHAPE UP

page 97

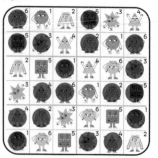

PJ PARTY FUN

page 98

COMPOUND CRITTERS page 99

1. bookworm 2. rainbow 3. jellyfish
4. dragonfly 5. watchdog 6. rattlesnake
7. toothbrush 8. carpool 9. flowerbed
10. bulldoze

TIME FOR SCHOOL

page 100

PENN SILL: Art at 10:30 am
MARK KERR: Music at 11:00 am
CAL Q. LATER: Library at 11:30 am
SHARPAY NERR: Phys Ed at 10:00 am

FISHY SUBTRACTION page 101

HOW MANY TICKLES DOES IT TAKE TO MAKE A JELLYFISH LAUGH? TEN TICKLES.

BRAIN BREAKS

pages 102–103

DO A WORD WORKOUT: The five real dinosaurs are *Brachiosaurus*, *Allosaurus*, *Apatosaurus*, *Iguanodon*, and *Megalosaurus*.
BE LOGICAL: Shape A fits the eggshell.
STRETCH YOUR MATH SKILLS: A STEGO-SNORE-US.

BEACH DAY page 105

WHAT'S BLACK AND WHITE AND RED ALL OVER? A SUNBURNED ZEBRA.
WHAT DO PIGS PUT ON THEIR SUNBURN? OINK-MENT.
WHAT IS THE BEST DAY TO GO TO THE BEACH? SUNDAY.

FAST FOOD pages 106–107

TIC TAC SHARKS

page 108

glasses round teeth speech bubble	glasses ice-cream cone	glasses hat polka dots
eyes closed round teeth	eyes closed ice-cream cone speech bubble polka dots	eyes closed hat
sweater round teeth polka dots	sweater ice-cream cone	sweater hat speech bubble

JUICY JOKES page 109

1. C 2. A 3. D 4. F 5. B 6. E

WOODLAND WHIMSY page 112

TOODLE-OO ZOO

page 113

1. BABOON 2. CROCODILE 3. BUFFALO
4. SHEEP 5. BUTTERFLY 6. KITTY CAT
7. GRIZZLY BEAR 8. CHIMPANZEE
9. RATTLESNAKE

SPELUNKING SPLENDOR pages 114–115

TOO MANY TACOS

page 116

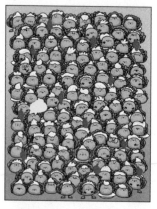

UNICORN ANIMALS

page 117

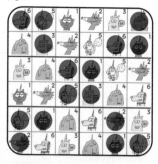

CANDY CHECK page 118

NO PROB-LLAMA

page 119

FUNNY FLOATS

page 120

1ST: Floaty McDuckface **2ND:** Seas the Day **3RD:** Keep Palm and Float On **4TH:** The Ripe Direction **5TH:** Doughnut Stop Me Now **6TH:** Flamingo-go-GO **7TH:** One in a Melon **8TH:** Her Royal Pine-ness **9TH:** Pizza My Heart

READY, SET, SLOW

page 121

SNAIL will arrive first in
3 hours (24 ÷ 8 = 3).
KOALA will arrive second in
4 hours (44 ÷ 11 = 4).
SLOTH will arrive third in
5 hours (30 ÷ 6 = 5).
TURTLE will arrive fourth in
6 hours (42 ÷ 7 = 6).
BONUS: Sloth used 73 items
(13 twigs, 24 shoots, and 36 leaves).

BRAIN BREAKS

pages 122–123

BE LOGICAL: Column B has five different shapes. Row 4 has five different colors.
DO A WORD WORKOUT: red, blue, green, purple, yellow
PLAY WITH PATTERNS: D has the most squares containing circles. B has the fewest squares containing triangles.

CRAWLY CRITTERS

page 125

WHAT BUG CAN TELL TIME?
A CLOCKROACH.
WHAT KIND OF INSECT IS BAD AT FOOTBALL? A FUMBLEBEE.
WHICH BUG NEVER DOES ITS CHORES? A LAZYBUG.
WHAT DO YOU CALL A MUSICAL INSECT? A HUMBUG.

SHARK-CUTERIE

pages 126–127

TIC TAC ALIEN

page 128

green desserts **triangle badge**	green purple hair	green two eyes nose on stalk
desserts pink background	purple hair pink background **triangle badge** nose on stalk	two eyes pink background
desserts teeth nose on stalk	purple hair teeth	two eyes teeth **triangle badge**

MERMAID MUSIC

page 132

BOX DROP page 133

WHAT DOES A SWEET POTATO WEAR TO BED? ITS YAMMIES.
BONUS:

SKI TRIP page 134

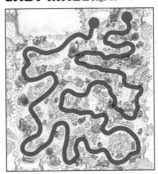

LAZY MAZE page 135

DUCK DUCK SWAN

page 136

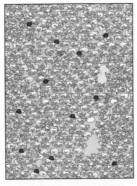

COMBO CUTIES

page 137

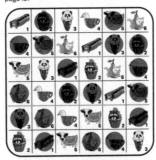

CATNAPPING pages 138–139

FUNGI PARTY page 140

PORTIA BELLA: streamers; petri hotdish
SHIA TAKI: balloons; fungus fudge
CHANTEL RELLE: party hats, puffball-roni pizza
MATT SUTAKI: candles, black forest cake

GOT A MINUTE? page 141

WHY WAS THE CLOCK SO LONELY?
IT HAD NO ONE TO TOCK TO.

BRAIN BREAKS

pages 142–143

TEST YOUR EYESIGHT: a bike helmet
DO A WORD WORKOUT: Altitude, Crosswind, Flaperon, Tailplane, Joystick, Rudder
BE LOGICAL: Fifteen cars
DECODE THE PUNCH LINE:
GO TO THE DOCK.

MATH MIRTH page 145

WHAT DO YOU CALL A FROG CAUGHT IN THE MUD? UNHOPPY.
WHAT IS A SNAKE'S FAVORITE SCHOOL SUBJECT? *HISS*-TORY.
WHAT DO YOU CALL A RICH LIZARD?
CHAMELEON-AIRE.

ALARM ANTICS

pages 146–147

TIC TAC AXOLOTL

page 148

teal and blue hat polka dots	teal and blue **stomach up**	teal and blue holding cup part of body teal
hat squiggly pattern	holding cup polka dots squiggly pattern **stomach up**	part of body teal squiggly pattern
sunglasses hat holding cup	sunglasses **stomach up**	sunglasses polka dots part of body teal

LOTL LETTERS: The two notes are I LOVE YOU ALOTL and GET SNAXOLOTLS.

MONSTER MATCH page 149

1. B, **2.** F, **3.** C, **4.** A, **5.** D, **6.** E

PLAY DAY! pages 150–151

Here's what we found. You may have found others: bee's sneeze, frog jog, dragon wagon, mole bowl, duck truck, snake cake, crab cab, frog log, maroon balloon, bug hug, swift gift, scuba tuba, flower power, cat hat, chimp blimp, train plane, kitten's mittens, snail mail

BURGER VS. FRIES

page 152

answers

LETTER DROP
page 153

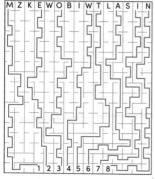

BONUS: WHAT DO YOU CALL A PILE OF CATS? A MEOW–TAIN.

MERMAID MAZE
pages 154–155

THERE ARE MORE CRABS THAN SEA STARS.

DOUGHNUT DASH
page 156

YOGA MOVES
page 157

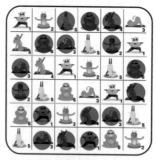

HAPPY FEET
page 158

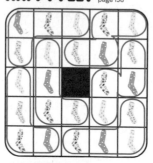

COMMANDER CACTUS
page 159

Here are the scenes in order: **E, G, I, B, A, F, D, H, C**

WHAT'S A FRUZZLE?
page 160

Fruzzles are smiling, are part or all green, and have one top blob.

GOING BANANAS
page 161

WHY DON'T BANANAS GET LONELY?
THEY ALWAYS HANG AROUND IN BUNCHES.

BONUS:
Why was the banana so popular?
[8, 8] [3, 1]   [9, 6] [6, 5] [3, 9]

[6, 5] [11, 9] [11, 9] [8, 1] [6, 5] [7, 9].

BRAIN BREAKS
pages 162–163

BE LOGICAL: Justin Thyme, Jean Yuss, Brock Lee, Clara Nett, Joe King, Crystal Ball, Mary Thon, Kara Mell, Al Dewitt
TEST YOUR EYESIGHT: a pickleball ball
DO A WORD WORKOUT: glove, ball, bat, net, clubs, cleats, skates, goggles, racket
STRETCH YOUR MATH SKILLS: The Seagulls scored 9, the Pelicans scored 6, the Seals scored 1, and the Loggerheads scored 0, for a total of 16 runs.

PRODUCE PARTY
page 164

HAVE AN ICE DAY!
page 165

BONUS: WE WENT THERE YESTERDAY. TODAY WE ARE GOING BOWLING!

BACK COVER

For information about permission to reprint selections from this book, please contact permissions@highlights.com.

Published by Highlights Press
815 Church Street
Honesdale, Pennsylvania 18431
ISBN: 978-1-63962-249-8
Manufactured in
Jefferson City, MO, USA
Mfg. 06/2024

First edition
Visit our website at Highlights.com.
10 9 8 7 6 5 4 3 2 1

Produced by WonderLab Group
Design: Nicole Lazarus
Photo Editor: Annette Kiesow

COVER ART BY SEBASTIAN ABBOUD

PHOTO AND ILLUSTRATION CREDITS: Sebastian Abboud (28, 133); Lindsey Baker (119); Tim Beaumont (103); Paula J. Becker (84, 135, 170); Kyle Beckett (106–107) Aaron Blecha (20, 159); Jim Bradshaw (3, 22–23, 43, 48, 63, 65, 108, 125, 166–169); Annika Brandow (16, 30, 70–71, 81, 121, 130–131); Cory Bugden (60); Mattia Cerato (55); Josh Cleland (103); Daryll Collins (26–27, 90–91); Catherine Copeland (58–59); Lee Cosgrove (132); Nichola Cowdery (148); Jana Curll (52, 92, 116, 134, 156, 164); Jef Czekaj (6–7, 74–75, 86–87); Luke Flowers (32, 126–127); Travis Foster (36, 56, 76, 96, 117, 136, 153); Getty Images (2, 3, 5, 9, 10–11, 13, 17, 18–19, 21, 22, 25, 29, 31, 33–34, 37, 38, 39, 40, 41, 42, 43, 45, 49, 57, 58–59, 61, 62, 63, 73, 77, 78, 80, 81, 82, 83, 85, 88, 89, 93, 97, 100, 101, 105, 109, 113, 118, 120, 122, 129, 138–139, 140, 142, 143, 145, 149, 157, 158, 161, 162, 163) Peter Grosshauser (8); Cedric Hohnstadt (163); Jango Jim/ Dimitri (98); Kelly Kennedy (4, 64); Annette Kiesow (123); Greg Kletzel (69); Gary LaCoste (23, 44, 46–47); Pat Lewis (72); Mike Lowery (12); Matt Lyon (137); Mike Moran (63, 162); Mitch Mortimer (23, 24, 104); Shaw Nielsen (114–115, 141, 150–151, 154–155); Neil Numberman (146–147); Garry Parsons (102); Gina Perry (66–67); Chris Piascik (99, 160); Rich Powell (83); Letizia Rizzo (54); Miguel Sanchez (152); Shutterstock (68, 165); Erica Sirotich (94); Scott Soeder (103); Amy Botticher Stroman (148); Jaka Vukotič (14–15, 42, 50–51, 53, 95); Brian Michael Weaver (35, 79); Michele Weisman (103); Tim Wesson/Alice (110–111, 128); Dave Whamond (124, 144); Pete Whitehead (122); Katie Wood (112)